# Remote Teaching and Learning:

## Reflections and Practical Advice

Magna Publications
Madison, Wisconsin

Magna Publications
2718 Dryden Drive
Madison, WI 53704
Magnapubs.com

Copyright © 2021 by Magna Publications

The articles in this book have been previously published in *The Teaching Professor* newsletter or the *Faculty Focus* blog.

ISBN: 978-0-912150-78-9

Compiled by Jon Crylen

# Contents

# Introduction

*Jon Crylen*

The articles assembled in this book were written between March 2020 and March 2021 and published in *The Teaching Professor* or *Faculty Focus*. All respond directly to the challenges of moving courses rapidly online during the COVID-19 pandemic. They speak to the experience of *emergency remote teaching*—a term that Hodges et al. (2020) coined early in the pandemic to describe "a temporary shift of instructional delivery to an alternate delivery mode due to crisis circumstances." This mode, they write,

> involves the use of fully remote teaching solutions for instruction or education that would otherwise be delivered face-to-face or as blended or hybrid courses and that will return to that format once the crisis or emergency has abated. The primary objective in these circumstances is not to re-create a robust educational ecosystem but rather to provide temporary access to instruction and instructional supports in a manner that is quick to set up and is reliably available during an emergency or crisis.

In other words, this is not a book about typical online teaching and learning, which educators have studied, practiced, and refined for decades. It is about stopgap pedagogy, about making do amid widespread uncertainty, exhaustion, and trauma. It is about effectively practicing a flawed mode of instruction to which we may not soon return. While several contributors to this collection are seasoned online faculty, their advice is less about running an effective, fully online course than using easy-to-implement online teaching techniques to make the best of a chaotic but ultimately transitory situation.

You may be wondering: If remote teaching isn't here to stay, then why publish (or read) a book on it? A few reasons come to mind.

First, the pandemic isn't over, and we don't know when it will end. The vaccine rollout is a cause for optimism, yes, but as of March 2021, we're a ways away from herd immunity. Another semester or two of at least partial remote teaching seems likely before campuses can safely reopen. In the interim, faculty can still benefit from others' guidance on managing in these unenviable conditions.

Second, we cannot rule out future transitions to remote learning. Hodges et al. note the likelihood of other public health crises as well as recent school closures resulting from natural disasters; certainly, the lengthier and more ferocious hurricane and wildfire seasons resulting from the accelerating climate crisis figure to interrupt at least some campus operations in the years ahead. It's also possible that choice rather than necessity may dictate online shifts, as when hazardous weather makes it safer and more convenient for classes to meet on Zoom. Whatever the case, articles in this book can assist faculty with remote teaching in a range of contingency scenarios.

Finally, this collection constitutes a partial record of how faculty responded to teaching during a global crisis—and how they tried to help their colleagues and their students through it. In this respect the book may seem of greater interest to historians of US higher education (as well as those studying COVID-19 pandemic response) than to teaching professors concerned with praxis. But I hope those faculty who visit these articles in calmer times can find flashes of inspiration and insight that shape how they approach teaching and learning challenges more mundane than a pandemic.

A note on the division of the book. Part 1: Reflections on Pandemic Teaching is ordered chronologically, with each successive article having been published deeper into the pandemic. These pieces tend to be specific to the past year, and to read them in sequence is, I hope, to engage with an evolving record of thought about teaching during a traumatic time. Part 2: Strategies and Practical Advice begins with a pair of articles written early during the pandemic but otherwise hews to no particular chronology. Entries here can aid readers at any stage of remote teaching; several of them double as primers on effective online teaching strategies that can benefit faculty who make forays into distance education proper. Lastly, Part 3: Resources for Students is what it sounds like: a set of notes and handouts that teachers can distribute to their students. Readers who wish to customize these can follow the links at the end of each piece to download an editable Word version of the text.

## Reference

Hodges, C., Moore, S., Lockee, B., Trust, T., & Bond, A. (2020, March 27). The difference between emergency remote teaching and online learning. *EDUCAUSE Review*. https://er.educause.edu/articles/2020/3/the-difference-between-emergency-remote-teaching-and-online-learning

# PART 1

# REFLECTIONS ON PANDEMIC TEACHING

# Teaching in Troubling Times

*Maryellen Weimer*

In the midst of the COVID-19 pandemic, as we deal with closed campuses and everything going online, we find ourselves teaching in the face of an array of circumstances that make learning difficult. The undercurrents of the unknown run deep. There are our own health concerns and those of the ones we love. There are financial worries. Will there be food in the grocery stores? How do we avoid getting on each other's nerves here at home? How long will this last? And finally, how do we teach when minds and hearts are a thousand places other than learning?

We can help students focus by providing the leadership that they've come to expect from us. Although we may feel inches from chaos, we do know how to teach, and we understand how students learn. That doesn't mean we ignore or downplay the challenges, but what's happening in the course—that's our bailiwick. Calm, steady leadership quiets panic and conveys confidence that we'll figure it out together.

Teaching under a new set of circumstances requires flexibility—the ability to respond to events on the fly. It's not a time for rigid standards and fixed policies or for clinging to how things have always been done. At this point, most of us have cobbled together a plan for what's going to happen in the course, but it's a work in progress and will evolve as circumstances change. We've unexpectedly been jolted off course, but we are still on the road and committed to doing what it takes to move the course forward.

Along with the uncertainty of the situation comes an opportunity to be with our students in different and deeper ways. Helping these students become a community of learners may be easier than it's been in any other course. As challenges emerge, we can talk about them! We can ask students to describe how problems look from their perspective and encourage them to share ideas, solutions, and other options. There's no need for social

distancing with remote teaching. In fact, it's a case for a close relation-
ship with the teacher and students working together in the face of shared
struggles.

It's not always bad for students to see teachers struggling with the details. My colleague Lolita was telling me stories the other day about her first
attempts with a synchronous online session—and she's an experienced online instructor. She was ready for her second set of PowerPoints, but where
were they? She clicked on icons and moved from screen to screen—her
face registering the disgust, frustration, and embarrassment she felt, forget-
ting that 40 students were looking on. With no PowerPoints, she had to
give up and end the session early, but with poise and grit in her voice she
announced that she would find them and do better next class session. I'll
bet students identified with her, comforted by the fact it's a trying time for
everyone.

The gift teachers most need to give themselves right now is space for a
less-than-best performance. Frustrating teaching experiences are filled with
potential for learning—for the teacher, yes, but also for the students who get
to see how a pro builds mistakes into a better performance. Instructors need
to occupy that space with humility but also with confidence. We are master
learners who know that mistakes are powerful teachers.

Teaching in troubling times opens up learning possibilities beyond
those the course provides. In compelling ways, we are making sense of our
priorities and seeing more clearly what really matters. Life is possible with
fewer than 24 rolls stashed in the bathroom. We are experiencing emptiness
without our communities—and grubby fullness with too much family.
But the absence and closeness of those most meaningful to us awakens the
frightful possibility of losing any of them. This is life on the edge with lessons ready for learning. All that's missing is a teacher.

# Flexibility: Where to Bend and How Much?

*Maryellen Weimer*

My recent column on teaching in troubling times mentions the need for flexibility, and one of my dear colleagues noted that the idea of flexibility needed to be fleshed out. I agree, with one of my first thoughts being I don't think I've ever read anything that explores how flexibility works in teaching situations.

In the natural world flexibility is tested in times of extremity. I live in the woods at the top end of a hollow that faces west. During storms the wind barrels through here, making the trees bend and branches twist and turn. Sometimes branches are ripped off, and occasionally a tree goes down, but most stay standing, ready to weather the next storm.

I'd say we're teaching in a storm right now—so we need to bend. But where do we bend and how much? Even though times are tough for everyone, it's hard for teachers not to feel caught in a bit of a bind. We do have standards to uphold, and students have been known to take advantage of teachers. We want to be flexible, but we also want the requests to make course changes and the asks for special accommodations to be legitimate. When we bend, we want to do so without damaging our ethical obligations as teachers.

Analyzing the situation starts simply enough. We can be flexible in two areas, the first being course-related issues. If something isn't working—whether the pace of the course, the online discussions, the access to resources, or the technology—it's pretty easy to ascertain whether that's a widespread problem. If so, then we can adjust with the goal of fixing the problem or at least making it better. It's more challenging to be flexible when standards are involved—say, to make an assignment easier or less complicated, cut the length, or extend the deadline. What circumstances justify those kinds of modifications?

Could we all agree? We've got to bend in the direction of learning. Instructional policies and practices must always and only be about learning. But the learning potential in a course is broad and doesn't always involve content. What if we opt not to discuss a set of assigned readings and instead ask whether the young have a responsibility to take actions that protect the old? Is that a bend in the direction of learning? Beyond course-level flexibility are those requests from individual students—for more time, for the chance to redo an assignment or make up a quiz, for extra credit, for counting effort—and those are much harder to sort out and through, especially in times of extremity. Does it make sense to take some time to think about the request before offering a response? Often the student request comes laden with emotion, which makes it easy to let emotion clutter the response. Am I saying yes because I want the student to think I'm a good person? Do I want to say yes because it's easier than saying no?

Beyond the most important consideration—what the request will do for the student's learning—there are fairness and equity issues. Course requirements should apply to all students equally, but does that mean all students must do the same things? Content can be learned in different ways, but different has a long history of not being equal. In this case, that's less because of bias than on account of the imprecision of grading measures. These issues are larger than any individual request, but they bubble up whenever a student asks us to be flexible about a requirement. Then again, bending in the direction of a student can make it easier to see how learning looks from that novice learner perspective.

If ever there was a time to be flexible, this is it. Our courses were interrupted and, in most cases, significantly altered midstream. We need to adjust and maybe in directions that make us stretch. It's a time of great anxiety, high stress, and fear for all of us. If ever we needed to be there for each other, that time is now. Teachers need students to be understanding, and students need teachers to be flexible for all sorts of good reasons. So we reach out. The wind blows, the tree bends and then straightens, rooted to the idea of holding on and standing tall.

# Pandemic Teaching Is Tough, but It Need Not Be Unexamined

*Regan A. R. Gurung*

I am not the same teacher I was six weeks ago.

Oh, I still care very much about my students. It is still very important to me that they are learning, that I help bring the content to life and make the material engaging and applicable. I want them to feel connected to me, their classmates, and the university (connections that synergistically help learning). It is just a lot harder to do. It takes a lot more conscious effort. I find that I am not automatically doing a lot of what was sine qua non of my modus operandi.

I feel exhausted most days. Somehow, even with no commuting, no ferrying two kids to practices and lessons, no grocery shopping, and no excursions into beautiful Oregon wilderness (don't get me started on how much I miss the coast, under an hour away), I still have less time and seemingly more work. With most of what we do in higher education already housed on computers, the now greater access to said screens can easily encroach on the time freed up by the inability to partake in normal activities. Research, writing, data analysis, and making a class better are all pursuits that, like a gas, expand to take the space you give it.

We may know the psychological story here. When organisms face unpredictable stressors over which they have little control and over a long duration, there is a toll on the psyche. Yes, personality traits such as optimism, self-esteem, resilience, and hardiness, as well as resources such as social support (both perceived and received), can alleviate some of the stress and the negative effects. Health behaviors such as eating well, not drinking too much, sleeping well, getting physical activity, and practicing mindfulness are excellent coping strategies too, nicely mediating the effects of stress on well-being. I remind myself that stress can take a toll even when we do not consciously recognize it. We all have to be watchful for those symptoms of implicit stress, those Zoomathon-inspired headaches, perhaps periods of helplessness, fatigue, and just sheer inability to function. Take your self-care up a notch. Bolster your natural capabilities by having coping activities to feature in your daily routines.

Slowly bandwidth will increase. As we habituate to the new normal, as we get more efficient at doing what we now do, as we consciously work to take care of ourselves and our loved ones, we will see gaps in the clouds, a way out of the seeming pits of despair.

Personally, my Emergency Remote Teaching has given way to Temporary Remote Teaching en route to Effective Blending Learning. At first the charge was to keep the lights on and teach a face-to-face course from afar. Time precluded a full course redesign. Some attempts resulted in Frankencourses or courses and a half (see Kahn, 2020, for a remote learning mix map that can prevent this), lumbering beasts of courses where face-to-face activities were mashed together with online courses, resulting in more work for students and teachers alike. There was undoubtedly some pruning of courses with many on-the-fly modifications. I found I used any moments of clarity to force myself to take a student perspective and adjust perhaps unreasonable requests or compensate for inadequate scaffolding and instructions.

Now, midway through, I am hitting my stride, cruising along in this temporary state of remote teaching. I am also looking ahead. I am coming to terms with new technological affordances, such as the abilities provided by breakout rooms, and am more open to leveraging the vast array of asynchronous course components to build community and increase student engagement. Previously the purview of online education, those of us taking our face-to-face classes into the cloud can benefit from best practices for using discussion rooms and more, focused around the useful categories of student-instructor, student-student, and student-content (see Riggs, 2020, for tips).

Be aware of nuances in language with significant implications as you approach the next few weeks and for when we may have to do this again. Rather than "online *lectures*," think about "online *classes*." What we are doing is not just taking our live lectures and recording them. *What we are doing is taking an entire face-to-face experience—blocks of time we spend with our students together in the learning process—and translating it into interactions shared through screens.* It is not only delivering content but also engineering a learning experience replete with opportunities for us and our students to interact with each other, apply and process material, and synthesize and create insights. That's not all; we are doing it in the face of students' perceptions (right and wrong) of what online learning is, their shock at being remote when expecting a face-to-face class, and their now idealized and potentially inaccurate sense of what was lost.

The challenge is to have pedagogically sound class time. This may mean untethering oneself from synchronous delivery. Yes, having a routine is useful, and many students who signed up for face-to-face classes may want and prefer fixed class times, but that may not be the most effective way for you to teach your course in your discipline. Online education is primarily asynchronous (hybrid and blended courses have some synchronous components). Consider variations on the theme where some meetings are synchronous. Reconsider what you do during those meetings. You may want to keep synchronous live meetings for discussion only and record short lectures that students can view asynchronously (they can still email questions and requests for clarification).

With a little more warning, once solely face-to-face instructors can now quickly adopt the best practices of online and blended learning. For example, at Oregon State University, we have a self-guided course on designing and modifying face-to-face courses for remote delivery. It is packed with helpful tips. The dust has settled on the pivot, and as responsible educators we need to prepare for the next step while also taking the time, mental health providing, to look at how our students are doing right now. We all know formative evaluations are particularly useful for students. This is the time to steel our resolve and carve out some time to see how we are doing. No one asked for this type of teaching and learning, but it does not mean we are powerless to do anything about it. There is still time for course corrections.

No, I am not the teacher I was six weeks ago, but after this all passes, I may be a better one.

**References**

Kahn, C. (2020, April 15). Be seen. Be heard. Teach effectively. *OSU Center for Teaching and Learning.* http://blogs.oregonstate.edu/osuteaching/2020/04/15/be-seen-be-heard-teach-effectively

Riggs, S. (2020, April 15). Student-centered remote teaching: Lessons learned from online education. *Educause Review.* https://er.educause.edu/blogs/2020/4/student-centered-remote-teaching-lessons-learned-from-online-education

**Further reading**

Amobi, F. (2020, April 20). Bringing out students' best assets in remote teaching: Questioning reconsidered. *OSU Center for Teaching and Learning*. http://blogs.oregonstate.edu/osuteaching/2020/04/20/bringing-out-students-best-assets-in-remote-teaching-questioning-reconsidered

Hahn, K. (2020, April 22). Getting close while teaching remotely: Instructor presence. *OSU Center for Teaching and Learning*. http://blogs.oregonstate.edu/osuteaching/2020/04/22/getting-close-while-teaching-remotely-instructor-presence

# Migratory Birds and the Written Word: Teaching Online during the Pandemic

*Katie E. O'Leary*

While domestic pigeons prove neighborhood nuisances in major cities, it's the common house sparrow who rattles rural areas. Look above the entrances to any apartment complex or office building in the Midwest, and you'll likely find reflective repellent to keep these birds from settling in public trestles. Some residents, like my neighbor—who from her balcony sprays sparrows with water—opt for a more personal approach. Ruthless and raucous, house sparrows deserve their reputation; comprising a global population of 540 million, they are one of the most invasive bird species in the world (Ackerman, 2016, p. 242).

Recent literature in nature and science, however, widely praises house sparrows for their unique ability to adapt to their surroundings. Unperturbed by human activity, these birds build their homes from nearly any type of man-made structure: porch lights, flowerpots, even the tailpipes of abandoned cars (Ackerman, 2016, p. 239). Moreover, house sparrows are exceptionally resourceful at gathering their nesting materials. When pliable grass and contour feathers cannot be found, household paper scraps and discarded cigarette butts work just fine. And it is their acute ability to adapt to their environment and tolerate change in their surroundings that has kept me, even as I write this, curiously watching them from my one-bedroom apartment—marking another week of a pandemic that seems to have left its mark on everyone and everything except that which is wild.

We hear the word *adapt* with increasing frequency lately. Social media posts and TV news anchors offer that now is the time to find our "new normal." And I think to some degree we in higher education feel that we need to find normalcy quickly. With over 100 students transitioning from my face-to-face classroom to online instruction, I think I've found the time to adapt, but this still doesn't feel at all normal. Because we are in such an unprecedented time, we don't yet know the effects this outbreak will have on us and our teaching—nor on our students and their learning. As a composition instructor, I also wonder about the extent to which my students' anxieties about writing will be compounded by this crisis. With so much uncertainty, it's overwhelming to figure out where to begin.

Students who have taken my composition courses know what I mean when I suggest, "bird by bird." I've quoted the phrase in emails, on chalkboards, and at the end of my students' papers. The title of a book by Anne Lamott, the motto has always grounded my approach to life and learning. Typically, around midterm, as my students are stressed by the weight of exams and have (admittedly) procrastinated on impending paper deadlines, I stand at the podium and offer Lamott's story:

> 30 years ago, my older brother, who was 10 years old at the time, was trying to get a report on birds written that he had 3 months to write, which was due the next day. We were at our family cabin in Bolinas, and he was at the kitchen table close to tears, surrounded by binder paper and pencils and unopened books on birds, immobilized by the hugeness of the task ahead. Then my father sat down beside him, put his arm around my brother's shoulder, and said, "Bird by bird, buddy. Just take it bird by bird." (Lamott, 1995, p. 19)

Lamott's point, in part, is to approach writing the same way: page by page, paragraph by paragraph, sentence by sentence, even word by word. The writing process can, at times, be recursive, messy, even overwhelming—especially when it's unfamiliar and new. And so that's how I frame Lamott's narrative for my first-year writing students.

It helps, too, that I occasionally share with my students my latest sightings. In addition to its population's share of the common house sparrow, Brookings, South Dakota, boasts a kind of bird-watching haven: great blue herons inhabit the nature park just outside of town, turkey vultures perch on Main Street's water tower, and red-winged blackbirds reside near campus and just recently announced their confident return. I like to think about how, at times, birds learn to adapt to the changing of seasons: searching for food in April blizzards and building nests out of nothing.

In this season of great uncertainty, I would posit that we as instructors can draw once more on our strengths as writers. Despite this new normal of video conferencing and prerecorded lectures, we can still approach teaching the same way we carry out our lives: one day at a time. Of course, students will disclose to us stressors that we are neither prepared for nor trained to address. They'll ask questions about technology. The internet will be slow, even fail for a time. But perhaps what we have now, more so than at the semester's beginning, is more time. Time to read. To listen. To explore the fricatives and fragments of language. To, as Anne Lamott suggests, take this bird by bird.

Songbirds like the bobolink sweetly harmonize across the open prairie, but wild geese are the chief harbingers of spring. Once considered extinct, geese mate for life and even experience distress when their flock is in trouble (Ackerman, 2016, p. 130). They form their migratory chevron shape by creating space behind and between each other. In doing so, they generate an "uplift": the airstream behind each goose that helps the entire flock travel farther together than if they were flying alone. Traversing long distances through unfavorable weather conditions, geese honk to communicate with and account for each member of their skein. But honking also serves as a form of social encouragement: not only to adapt their pace, but to maintain space—to uplift. And as we navigate this new season with our students and colleagues, so, too, shall we.

## References

Ackerman, J. (2016). *The genius of birds*. Penguin.

Lamott, A. (1995). *Bird by bird: Some instructions on writing and life*. Knopf Doubleday.

# Meeting the Expectations of Post-pandemic Students

*Robert S. Fleming*

In recent weeks, faculty members and their institutions across the nation and around the world have embraced the necessity of transitioning their courses to various remote delivery modes. While most faculty members have had to make some accommodations in their current courses, the necessity of moving to remote course delivery was particularly challenging for faculty who had not previously developed or delivered online courses. Fortunately, with support and assistance from administrators and staff, as colleagues we have and continue to work together to ensure that our students will be able to complete their courses and stay on track for graduation.

For many students, this worldwide pandemic may be the first real crisis that they have experienced. It's easy to forget that most of our students were either not yet born at the time of the September 11 terrorist attacks or too young to understand them. Students enrolled in my business capstone courses that semester tell me how they remember that we had assigned organizations for their consulting projects the day before the attacks and how the world in which we live, work, and travel changed forever the next day. In class the day after the attacks we engaged in the first of a series of discussions that continued throughout the semester as we considered the challenges of various crises to the survival and continued success of an organization.

While our current students may not remember the events of September 11, they are living the COVID-19 pandemic. It has clearly changed all aspects of our world, including how we, as educators, continue to prepare our students for successful personal and professional futures.

Who would have imagined a time when college and university employees would be encouraged—if not told—to stay away from our campuses for most of a semester and now at many institutions through the summer?

Planning for the upcoming academic year will be more challenging than usual. When it will be practical to resume in-person instruction is also unknown. While there are many things we do not know now and may not know for some time, there is one reality that we should acknowledge: our students will share the common experience of the devastating current pandemic. We need to recognize this and respond appropriately as we, as post-pandemic faculty, prepare and deliver courses to our post-pandemic students.

While in recent weeks we have rightly focused on making a successful transition to remote course delivery, we should now begin to consider how and when to incorporate reflection on the events of this pandemic in our respective classes. While there will obviously be courses where these discussions would probably not be relevant, there are likely more courses than may at first be apparent where it could certainly be appropriate and beneficial to consider the implications of the COVID-19 pandemic. The relevance of courses designed to prepare business, communications, journalism, medical, psychology, social work, and public relations professionals stand out among the many potential courses where students could benefit from studying the current and other crises through experiential learning activities. The perspective of our various disciplines and programs can deepen students' understandings of the wide-ranging effects of the pandemic.

As important as the question of how we will deliver courses that provide effective, efficient, and safe instruction is, we should not become so preoccupied with the delivery mode that we fail to take the opportunity at this crucial juncture to consider relevant course updates that align with the "new normal" that our graduates, their professions, and organizations will face in a post-pandemic world. While our recent focus has been on transition, we now have a strategic opportunity to transform the courses we teach to better prepare our graduates for the many challenges of a constantly evolving world. Our commendable accomplishments in recent weeks demonstrate what we can do in a crisis situation. We can certainly rise to the challenge revising course content, assignments, and activities so that they reflect what we have learned about what students now need to know.

Our graduates and the organizations for which they will work expect that our academic programs will prepare them appropriately to embrace and enact their professional responsibilities. If we did not realize it before, the recent crisis events have taught us the important role that various professions play in preventing, responding to, mitigating, and recovering from crises. Now is thus the time to transform our courses to incorporate relevant, discipline-oriented crisis management lessons. There may also be opportunities for value-added interdisciplinary collaboration. Our post-pandemic students expect and deserve nothing less!

# Certainties amid Uncertainty

*Maryellen Weimer*

Most of us are not feeling the anticipation we usually feel at the beginning of a new academic year. Anxiety is closer to what most of us are experiencing. What's going to happen when the students come back to campus—or when they don't? How bad are finances at the institution? Are cuts to jobs or programs a possibility? Will the semester end as it began? With so much up in the air, I wondered whether it would help to review what we know for sure—certainties in these times of uncertainty.

**We've got students who need teachers**, even more than they usually do. Growing up isn't easy, never has been, but the uncertainties add another layer. For older students, heading back to school with life already in full swing is always challenging, but now issues at home and work add more complications. But the reasons students opt for school haven't changed. They're after the credentials that structured learning opportunities provide. Everything we teach can be learned without us, but the vast majority of students learn more and learn it better when a teacher guides the process. Yes, right now we're doing more hand-holding than usual, but what students most need are models of how educated persons act in times of uncertainty—that quiet calm; the reasoned, thoughtful response; the confidence that we'll figure it out; and the conviction that we'll prevail in the course, in college, and beyond. With so much up in the air, students need us to help them stay grounded.

It may be a year of unknowns, but **we start it knowing how to teach**. Some of us have miles of experience behind us, and others may not have been on the road for long. All of us, however, are sophisticated learners who understand what teachers can do to aid the learning process. We can explain things, provide examples, ask questions, answer questions, rephrase, refute, summarize, document, provide lists, and draw from our repertoire a host of other teaching behaviors that pave the road to learning. We don't always teach perfectly. Our teaching remains a work in progress, but we can still trust ourselves. This fall our job is to teach. That hasn't changed, and it's something we know how to do.

Then **there's our content—we know it**, in most cases love it, and are firmly convinced of its inherent worth. How many of us announce with conviction that the material in the course we are about to teach contains some of the most important content students will learn in college? And the uncertainties of 2020 haven't changed that. Moreover, is there anything we teach from which larger lessons cannot be extracted—lessons with relevance to what we're experiencing in the pandemic, as a country, on the planet, and in our daily lives?

**We've got colleagues who care**, if not next door then no further than a text away. We're not starting a new academic year alone. The uncertainties are shared. We grapple with an array of changing circumstances together. In more settled times, most of our instructional knowledge we glean from each other. Research consistently confirms that. With new instructional issues emerging, we need to rely on our collective abilities to solve problems, learn from mistakes, and collaborate on creative solutions. And when anxiety and pessimism fester inside, we can turn to each other for the advice and support we need to carry on. Our colleagues who care will be there for us, just as we will be there for them.

Finally, **we've got a mission that matters**: we're educators! What a role education has to play when uncertainty surrounds us—it fills the need for reasoned discourse, develops the ability to sort fact from fiction, establishes the value of multiple perspectives, promotes respect for all, and legitimizes challenging assumptions. The current crisis will be resolved, most likely by a vaccine developed by persons with an education. Equally compromising issues, problems, and crises will emerge in our students' futures, and in those uncertain situations there'll be the same urgent need for educated answers.

No, it's not the academic year we'd choose, but it's the one that's ahead of us. While uncertainty abounds, it's tethered to powerful forces that will pull us through. This year holds all the promise and potential of every new academic year. They are yours to realize.

# Looking for Learning in the Transition to Online Courses

*Maryellen Weimer*

As Regan Gurung pointed out in his May 2020 article ("Pandemic Teaching Is Tough, but It Need Not Be Unexamined"), teaching during the pandemic merits analysis. The fast transition to online instruction was terribly challenging and not to be repeated (we can only hope). And although learning how to respond during a pandemic is important, what may be more enduring is discovering what happens to education when online courses are the norm.

I will grant that looking back at the spring semester with any sort of objectivity is tough. For many of us (both teachers and students), it's not a view that showcases teaching and learning at their best. And for that we should feel no guilt; we did the best we could during an extremely difficult time. Furthermore, the pandemic itself brought uncertainty, fear, and a plethora of problems. Without doubt, those influenced what happened in our courses, and their effects can't easily be sorted out.

Even so, it's worth taking a look with whatever objectivity we can muster. And I'm seeing any number of articles in the pedagogical periodicals that are doing just that. Here are highlights from three published in October that, in addition to providing insights on remote instruction, can help us put some perspective on our individual experiences.

Besser and colleagues (2020) wanted to better understand how students responded to the abrupt transition to online learning. Most of us will not be surprised that when asked to compare learning experiences in the course before and after the change, the 1,217 students surveyed reported "pervasive negative reactions to the online condition," including significantly lower levels of positive mood, relatedness, concentration and focus, motivation, and performance. Garris and Fleck (2020) asked 482 undergraduates to each evaluate a course that transitioned online, and students rated those courses as less enjoyable, less interesting, lower in learning value and levels of attention, and having less cultural content than face-to-face courses.

Gurung and Stone (2020) tried to fine-tune these typical student responses. They surveyed 649 students in 11 sections of introductory psychology, and they explored how students' preferences for online or face-to-face learning affected ratings of their learning in the online portion of the course, the study behaviors they reported using, and their achievement in the course. "Students who believed they did not perform well in online classes scored lower on final exams, on all measures of perceived learning in the class, and also reported the biggest changes in their learning behaviors during the pandemic."

Not all the findings in these three studies were bleak. Bresser et al. used a modified adaptability scale developed in previous research and found that students who scored high on adaptability reported higher positive mood scores and lower loneliness scores. "The apparent advantages of adaptability extended to higher reported levels of attention and focus, greater depth of learning, and indices reflecting greater motivation to learn." Being able to adapt is an important skill, and it's one that can be taught.

Gurung and Stone measured students' "modality based self-efficacy" or their beliefs about their ability to succeed in face-to-face and online courses. Students' levels of self-efficacy predicted final exam scores and their ratings of the skills learned. In the Garris and Fleck study, self-efficacy predicted higher course evaluations. Here, too, teachers can be instrumental in helping students develop beliefs about their capabilities.

So far I've yet to see any descriptive analyses of teachers' experiences and assessments of the switch. There are lots of promising accounts of technology-reluctant teachers confronting and conquering the technology needed to teach online. Garris and Fleck report that "instructor confidence with transitions online impacted students' evaluation of course quality." If the instructor communicated confidence, that predicted "favorable evaluations of each of the dimensions of course quality." Their student cohort also reported that they experienced greater flexibility in the transitioned courses. Teachers worked harder to accommodate special needs and institutions revised policies, making pass-fail options available, for example.

Widespread use of online learning modalities did once again raise questions about the continuing use of these courses. The power of student preferences shown in the Gurung and Stone study raises the ongoing and largely unanswered question of who should take online courses. Only those students who choose to? Are some kinds of content better suited for online delivery? If so, what kinds? Who should be teaching online—only those teachers who choose to? Our recent experiences make this a particularly good time to talk about online instruction.

**References**

Besser, A., Flett, G. L., & Zeigler-Hill, V. (2020). Adaptability to a sudden transition to online learning during the COVID-19 pandemic: Understanding the challenges for students. *Scholarship of Teaching and Learning in Psychology*. Advance online publication. http://dx.doi.org/10.1037/stl0000198

Garris, C. P. & Fleck, B. (2020). Student evaluations of transitioned-online courses during the COVID-19 pandemic. *Scholarship of Teaching and Learning in Psychology*. Advance online publication. http://dx.doi.org/10.1037/stl0000229

Gurung, R. A. R., & Stone, A. M. (2020). You can't always get what you want and it hurts: Learning during the pandemic. *Scholarship of Teaching and Learning in Psychology*. Advance online publication. https://doi.org/10.1037/stl0000236

# Riding the Wheel of Fortune: How the Substance of Our Teaching can Help us through the Crisis

*Joseph Bentz*

Much of the discussion about the move to remote and online classes this school year has focused on the mechanics of such teaching—how to make online learning engaging, how to create community, how to use the technology better. But what about the *substance* of what we are teaching? How can the actual content of the courses help students and faculty better understand and cope with the upheaval into which their lives have been thrown? Good teaching is not just about getting the technology right. It's also about having something to *say*, something worth showing up for.

In one of my Honors College courses at Azusa Pacific University, for example, we read *The Consolation of Philosophy*, written by Boethius in 525 CE. What could a Roman government official from 1,500 years ago possibly have to offer 20-year-old college students today? This book has a pointed, direct message for the crisis in which we are living, regardless of whether we discuss it together in person or on Zoom.

Boethius writes about the Wheel of Fortune, not in the modern, TV-game-show sense of that term but in an older way of understanding it. Boethius's Wheel of Fortune does not spin around and land on expensive prizes. A human being—you—rides Boethius's Wheel. One spin of the Wheel may put you at the top, with everything going your way, but then the next spin thrusts you to the bottom, upside down, barely hanging on. Fortune—or Lady Fortuna—is fickle. She doesn't owe you anything. She may smile upon you one second and betray you the next.

Boethius lived much of his own life at the top of Fortune's Wheel. He grew up in a powerful family, married well, moved quickly up the political ladder, became a respected scholar and writer, and raised sons who also became powerful leaders. He had it all, but then suddenly, because of political machinations and one bad spin of the Wheel, he lost it all. He found himself unfairly imprisoned without trial; stripped of his wealth, power, and freedom; and ultimately tortured and executed.

He was shocked and bewildered at this sudden turn of events. How could it happen? What did it mean? What implications did it have for the philosophy and faith on which he had built his life? What should he do about it? What should he think about it?

The result of agonized thinking became his most famous work, *The Consolation of Philosophy*. Students today may not be facing Boethius's fate, but most of them will relate to someone who had his life upended through no fault of his own. Students are not living the college experience they thought was theirs. They are cut off from friends, from their college social lives, from job opportunities, from sports and other extracurricular pursuits, from those chance encounters that lead to unexpected friendships, romances, and connections that may last a lifetime. They didn't do anything to deserve this. They ask the same questions Boethius asked. Why? What meaning does this disruption have? What happens next?

Faced with this unwelcome turn of Fortune, Boethius turns to what I tell my students they might ultimately rely on: his education. He had spent his life studying the great philosophers and religious thinkers and texts. Now he turns to them again—with urgency.

Coping with their own crisis, students can decide to use what they are learning for a much more important purpose than simply getting a good grade: they can use the reading to make sense of their lives. Much of the *Consolation* is a dialogue between Boethius and a character he calls Lady Philosophy. In a sense, when Boethius talks to Lady Philosophy, he is talking to himself, the part of him that is trying to make sense of things while the Boethius part of him agonizes. Lady Philosophy also represents the Greco-Roman-Christian philosophy that Boethius knew so well. When he first learned it, however, life was good, and much of what he learned was of more interest at the intellectual level rather than the gut level. Now, he has to look at that philosophy anew to see if it *really* works when life turns sour.

I tell my students that as they go through their education, they are creating their own Lady Philosophy. Some of it may be relevant immediately, but the rest of it may sit in their minds for years before life's circumstances force them to recall it and test its truth. Better to create a Lady Philosophy who has something to say in those dire moments than to ignore their education and be left without resources when the Wheel of Fortune turns downward.

So what does Lady Philosophy have to say to the traumatized Boethius? Like students in a pandemic, he first needs time to complain, so Lady Philosophy simply *listens* to him for a while. He is in no condition to hear easy answers—or even hard answers. He needs time to mourn, and she gives it to him. There is great wisdom in that, my students realize. In the midst of grief and disappointment, quick answers, even if they're philosophically correct, only bring resentment.

As she gently leads him forward, she does so with questions that help him to challenge his own false assumptions. Fortune is fickle, and he should not assume that he somehow *deserves* only good fortune and must never accept the bad. It's a mistake to put his trust in fleeting values, such as wealth, power, and honors, which can so quickly evaporate.

Even in the best of times, the idea of reaching complete satisfaction is an illusion. Lady Philosophy says, "Man's condition produces anxiety; it never proves wholly satisfactory; it never lasts forever" (p. 42). Lady Philosophy pushes Boethius away from finding his identity in external satisfactions such as clothes, jewelry, mansions, and fame, and she urges him toward values that last, such as goodness, faith, and a belief in God's providence. She asks, "Are you so impoverished that you have no innate good that belongs to you? Must you seek your good in things that are external and not your own?" (p. 49). Lady Philosophy does not solve Boethius's outward crisis. He remains imprisoned and eventually is executed. But she does help him come to terms with his internal crisis. She brings him a new perspective on his situation, a new peace and contentment in spite of circumstances.

Without the crisis, would he ever have deeply questioned his values, behaviors, and false assumptions? I wish the pandemic of our own day had never happened. Like my students, I would love nothing more than to be where I was a year ago, gathered in a classroom with other human beings, talking about the texts and enjoying one another's presence. This is a time filled with anxiety and disappointment. We may be at the bottom of the Wheel, but sometimes it is at the bottom where we can learn the most.

**Reference**
Boethius. (2012). *The consolation of philosophy* (S. Goins & B. H. Wyman, Trans.). Ignatius Press. (Original work published ca. 524 CE)

# The Magic of Synchrony in Coping with Remote Learning

*Regan A. R. Gurung*

As fall 2020 draws to a close, the reactions to remote learning are reverberating loudly. They include not only outrage and despondency but also gratefulness and appreciation. Student surveys taking the pulse of learning experiences look very much like the evaluations of teaching we in higher education are used to seeing. The comments go both ways, but there is one unique element. We glimpse the value of synchrony—the opportunity for live synchronous meetings, even if they're remote.

First, the recap. One group of students does not like how learning management systems (LMSs) were set up, the frequency with which faculty respond to emails, the amount of work assigned, and the lack of flexibility and compassion displayed in the face of coping with a pandemic. Another group of students praises faculty for how LMSs were set up, the frequency with which they responded to emails, the amount of work assigned, and the flexibility and compassion displayed in the face of coping with a pandemic. Given the variance in importance placed on teaching across departments and campuses, the level at which it is evaluated in promotion and tenure, and the corresponding instructor training and faculty development, the spectrum of comments should surprise no one.

From a pedagogical standpoint, the story remains the same: be clear, compassionate, organized, multifaceted, flexible, and engaging (CCOMFE; Gurung, 2020). There are clear, evidence-informed principles for teaching that should be followed now as always. What has changed is that faculty and universities in general are paying more attention to the student experience. This is a good thing, and we need to capitalize on it. Before COVID-19, it was predominantly online courses that were scrutinized even after requiring instructors to first take significant training before teaching and working with an instructional designer. Remote teaching reminds us that all teaching, especially face-to-face teaching, needs the same attention, training, support, and reward structure. A critical element of face-to-face teaching is the amount of contact time and in particular the synchronous nature of class time. This is a good time to consider the value of synchronicity.

I taught general psychology remotely this term to nearly 300 students. I read all about different ways to optimize Zoom, use breakout rooms, and structure each class period (all courtesy of some great work from the staff of our Center for Teaching and Learning, Academic Technology, and Ecampus). Near every class period, I used most of the tools available including well placed polls and Google Docs to make student collaborations visible (and allow me to provide participation points). I urged students to turn cameras on if they were comfortable and use the chat for questions and comments. I did not penalize lack of camera use, and I recorded and posted lectures for those who could not make it or who wanted to go over points again.

So how did it go? Some days were a comedy of errors. I would share the wrong screen (my notes rather than the slides), have camera fails and sound lags, and feel like I was not connecting with students, technology aside. We also had many good times. We shared pictures of our pets and discussed good streaming shows during breaks, and sometimes childcare went on simultaneously. Attendance was high, and even as it dropped, by midterm over 70 percent showed up before going to 60 percent the last few weeks of school. Ironically, this pattern seemed even better than in some face-to-face terms. Did I benefit from a general need for connection? Perhaps. Students reported coming to class to see each other and, in particular, take part in the live chat. They knew when they could see friendly faces and engage in intellectual exchanges—the benefits of synchrony.

Delivering live lectures via Zoom at first seemed daunting. The first day of having rows of windows of cameras on screen and participants in the high three digits was a wild ride. The abundance of live students (mostly) sitting there while I stood in my home office, alone in person but virtually mobbed, was a surreal experience. But it made a difference. It felt electric. It felt vibrant. Because we were all *there* together. Even a class session peppered by questions in chat, the occasional voices on mike (either on purpose or by mistake), and by the tangents allowed by being present together, all underscored the benefits of being live. The cadence of my speech, the pacing of delivery, and the very existence of discussion made possible by virtue of synchrony, provided much of the semblance of what education is when face-to-face. As students attested, having a live lecture also helped *them* focus and pay attention, akin to sitting in a physical classroom. They felt like active participants in the creation of knowledge.

Midterm evaluations suggested many students were having a positive experience. Scores on my first exam were similar to my first exam scores pre-pandemic. Of course, this does not mean I or students want more remote teaching. Most do not, and many have significant reservations about it. Research conducted by my applied cognition lab in real classrooms this spring show that students' perceived levels of self-efficacy for remote learning significantly predicted their exam scores. In a paper in *Scholarship of Teaching and Learning in Psychology*, my coauthor Arianna Stone and I show that in addition to the problems with expecting one will not do well, the mismatch between one's preferred modality for learning (face-to-face or online) is a significant predictor of less learning (Gurung & Stone, 2020). This does not mean students in general learn less during remote learning. A comparison of spring 2020 and fall 2019 exam scores did not show significant differences.

Nobody wants the pandemic to go on. Yet teaching during a pandemic has revealed a lot about how higher education works. It has laid bare course design and technology shortcomings (especially in the case of LMSs), resulting in student and faculty distress, while highlighting these same strengths for students with positive experiences. Both faculty and students have missed the concrete reality of meeting face-to-face and all that goes with it, even the daily commutes, the squeaky chairs, the sounds of metal thermoses rolling along floors, or the crinkle of a neighbor's snacks. We have all needed new routines, and while we made them, they came with fewer changes in scenery, with those at both ends of the screens often limited to the confines of the same four walls. But in all this we have had each other. Faculty and students meeting live multiple times per week have still had that chance to create knowledge via mutual interaction. The magic of synchrony is what will help us make it through to the end.

## References

Gurung, R. A. R. (2020, June 10). Pandemic teaching prescriptions. *Inside Higher Ed.* https://www.insidehighered.com/advice/2020/06/10/six-factors-best-online-experiences-faculty-and-students-share-opinion

Gurung, R. A. R., & Stone, A. M. (2020). You can't always get what you want and it hurts: Learning during the pandemic. *Scholarship of Teaching and Learning in Psychology.* Advance online publication. https://doi.org/10.1037/stl0000236

# A Skull, a Screen, and a Quarantine: Teaching Shakespeare during the Pandemic

*Nichole DeWall*

In more than a decade of teaching *Romeo and Juliet* at my small liberal arts college, I'd never had a student walk through class wearing only a towel. Then again, I'd never taught Shakespeare during a pandemic before.

Like many first-time remote instructors, I prepped my fall semester by researching best practices in synchronous online education, fretting about bandwidth and Zoom fatigue. But while my colleagues agonized over being so far away from our students, I worried about the opposite: that Zoom teaching brought us too close.

For all its usefulness, we've learned that Zoom is very bad at keeping secrets, and that concerned me. I was neither interested in my students' secrets nor particularly keen to share mine. I knew my students would Zoom in from spaces that in pre-pandemic times they'd kept private: dorms, cars, locker rooms, and family homes. I was planning to teach from my bedroom while my two young children attended virtual school from makeshift workspaces in our house. Without the more neutral space of the classroom, it all felt way too personal.

You see, I've never been the kind of professor who knows much about her students' personal lives. While I enthusiastically support their public endeavors—concerts, athletic events, thesis presentations—I don't often know who they're dating, what they post on social media, or what they do after hours. My students and I tend to form lasting connections by reading great literature together.

Likewise, I don't share much about my private life beyond the occasional anecdote. My ability to be discrete, of course, is a marker of privilege: I don't have a visible disability that divulges itself to the world without my consent, and the luxury of steady childcare ensures that my kids never accompany me to work. During my two pregnancies, I resented my swelling body for broadcasting my private business to my classes. When my students organized a baby shower for me, I was touched by the gesture; inwardly, though, I cringed.

As an assistant professor—newly minted, young, and female—I was advised against becoming too chummy with my students: "Don't try to be their friends," a colleague warned, "you'll lose all authority." Perhaps I inherited a certain stoicism from my Scandinavian ancestors, or as a Gen-Xer I'll never understand my students' generational embrace of self-revelation.

In truth, I am envious of my colleagues' more casual relationships with our students and their seemingly effortless abilities to move fluidly between their professional and private selves. They pepper their lectures with personal stories of loss, persistence, and joy. My colleagues adorn their offices with family photos and their kids' artwork; my well-worn facsimile of the First Folio is the most personal object on display in mine.

It's no wonder, then, that the idea of Zoom teaching felt so uncomfortable: it threatened to rupture my careful seal between work and home. "I feel like teaching from home will humanize me," a colleague said. I nodded, and wondered what I was missing. What I did miss was the liminal stillness of my commute through the rural Illinois countryside. I missed feeling the quiet morning calm of campus give way to the scuttle and rush of students. I longed for the small rituals of the classroom: a backpack unzipping, a pencil poised, a book spine splaying. Above all, I missed the cathedral-like hush that descended upon us when we read out Shakespeare's words.

I attempted to make new rituals. I commandeered a corner of our bedroom and staged it with bookshelves and a few select objects: Yorick's skull, the Droeshout portrait. If my space looked enough like my campus office, my students wouldn't sense the basket of dirty laundry or unmade bed just a few feet away. In a few weeks, I thought, I would forget how unnatural this all feels.

Teaching is performative; as a Shakespearean, I am undismayed by the notion that we are all actors on the world's stage. As my students tentatively filtered into our Zoom classroom on the first day, I was determined to play the role of The Before Times Professor: rigorous, professional, and competent.

But it became clear after the first week that my students needed something different from me. They were at sea. They needed connections, not complications. They needed a professor who was more open, more vulnerable: a Falstaff, not a Henry IV.

And so I adapted. I forced myself to get personal. I shared my fears about the rising coronavirus cases in our area. I asked students to introduce me to their pets, children, and roommates. They lounged around on their beds, Zoomed in from their (parked) cars, and attended sessions during their breaks at McDonald's. "I put up a 'Do Not Disturb' sign for our writing conference," a student revealed one afternoon, sheepishly, "but . . . well . . ." His voice trailed off. It was clear from his roommates' game of *Grand Theft Auto* in the background that his request had gone unheeded. "No biggie," I said, and reminded him of our newly adopted class mottos: "Come as you are" and "Embrace the weirdness." My students were doing their best, and their efforts were commendable.

Before COVID-19, I dismissed get-to-know-you games as wastes of time; now I scoured the internet for virtual icebreakers. I let my students choose which pair of Shakespeare-themed socks I wore and polled them about their favorite Thanksgiving foods. One morning, I asked my 10-year-old son to recite Puck's epilogue for the class. When my seven-year-old misplaced the password to one of her many e-learning apps, I stepped away briefly; my students understood. I exhaled.

The pandemic, of course, had a way of making everything personal. As the virus stalked closer to our small Midwestern town, my students and I braced for impact. My students' parents, siblings, and grandparents lost their jobs or got sick. Together, we bore witness to the horrors of human frailty. The morning that preliminary vaccine efficacy data were released, we cheered in celebration.

The virus didn't care about my students' precious college experiences. Despite my university's best efforts, some of my students became sick and quarantined during the semester. Most of them made full recoveries, but one infected student confessed that she'd lost vision in her left eye. My heart sank. "I'm so sorry that this is happening to you," I said, and instinctively placed my hand on my screen. She smiled back anxiously.

After that first week, I made a conscious decision to adopt a new teaching persona, one who turned away from complicating Shakespeare and leaned into my students' connections to the plays. Instead of focusing on A *Midsummer Night's Dream*'s allegorical references to Queen Elizabeth, my students were drawn to Titania's plague-infested forest and its altered seasons. This upside-down world resonated with them like never before.

When we reached *Hamlet*'s churchyard scene, I held my plastic skull up to the camera. While students peered into Yorick's hollow sockets, we talked of our pandemic's memento mori: refrigerated morgue trucks, intubators, and N95 masks. Even so, we managed a few laughs. Prince Hal's conflict between the Boar's Head Tavern and his father's court was my students' conflict too: "He just wants to go out and have a beer with his buddies," one student remarked, sighing, "I can totally relate." When Friar John is quarantined in *Romeo and Juliet*, a student exclaimed, "No wonder the play feels apocalyptic! They're in the middle of a pandemic, too!" "Excellent point," I affirmed. "I guess Romeo and Juliet forgot about that whole social distancing thing, huh?," another student quipped. Pandemic humor.

I worried that my students' experiences in my class were not as robust or rigorous as their pre-pandemic peers'. But perhaps this semester had revealed the immense generosity of Shakespeare's work. The plays expanded, contracted, and accommodated. They were always just what we needed them to be.

I harbor no illusions that one semester of pandemic teaching will radically change who I am as a professor or as a person. I will probably never decorate my campus office with family pictures or connect with students on social media. Going forward, though, I will try to better understand my students' needs, even if doing so feels uncomfortable at first. It took a once-in-a-century pandemic to show me just how full my students' lives are, and I won't soon forget that lesson.

During our last class, I intended to deliver inspirational remarks about the persistence of the human spirit and the power of the humanities; instead, I simply told my students what an honor it was to be their teacher. They each waved goodbye from their little gray box, and I took a moment to capture this final pandemic tableau in my mind's eye. Then I logged off.

# PART 2

# STRATEGIES AND PRACTICAL ADVICE

# Taking Your Classes Online in a Flash

*John Orlando*

Most higher education institutions have put their classes online for the remainder of the term. Higher education is well positioned to take classes online because so much of teaching in higher education is lecture driven rather than reliant on one-on-one interactions as in the K–12 realm. Additionally, nearly all schools already have a learning management system (LMS) on hand. Here are some tips for moving classes online in a flash.

### Use video conferencing to lecture, but mix up your delivery

Most institutions will use the LMS they already have to move classes online. Instructional designers will work with you to move the assessments, quizzes, and other resources into the courses. Your biggest job will be creating the lectures.

The easiest method of putting lectures online is with live video conferencing. Nearly all LMSs have built-in video conferencing ability, and if it is not available on your school's particular LMS, you can use Zoom, WebEx, or Google Hangouts. The free version of Zoom has some limitations that make it less than ideal for faculty, such as a 40-minute limit on meeting length, so I would use it only if your institution provides a premium version. Cisco is making WebEx free to any school and even provides guides for faculty and students on how to use it. Hangouts is another excellent free alternative that is entirely browser based and rarely has compatibility issues with student or faculty computers. Students merely need a URL and can log on at the same time as the faculty member.

It is important to keep in mind that online teaching is generally not live, and broadcasting yourself by webcam or your notes by PowerPoint is not the best means of delivering content online. The format is used here only due to the time constraints of a rapid transition. Real online teaching involves content developed for a web format, such as the digital storytelling model of narration combined with imagery and videos, much like a documentary or the better YouTube educational content.

But given a lack of time to create real online content, broadcasting yourself speaking is your best option. What should these lectures contain? You may be tempted to simply speak to a webcam the entire time. If you use PowerPoint in your regular lectures, you may want to broadcast your slides while you speak. Either will work in a pinch, but neither is ideal. Nobody wants to watch a talking head for more than a few minutes, and "death by bullet point" limits an audience's attention to about five minutes at most.

Instead, consider interspersing outside resources such as YouTube videos or TED Talks into your lectures every five to 10 minutes. My motto: "If someone can say it better than you, then let them." Faculty teaching face-to-face assume that they need to create all the educational content themselves, but online faculty know that there is a world of exceptional content out there waiting to be used. This is an opportunity to expose traditional faculty to that content, which they might end up using in their face-to-face classes next term.

Putting lectures online is trickier in quantitative fields that require instructors to work through equations. For these courses, one option is set up a camera in a classroom and record yourself speaking in front of the blackboard if your school is still open, though it might be hard to find an audio-visual person with the time to record you. A better option, if available, is to ask your institution for a tablet or touchscreen laptop that you can draw on and screencast during your lectures using Zoom, Google Hangouts, or Screencast-O-Matic or borrow one from somebody else.

### Try Google Classroom

If your institution is one of the few that lacks an LMS or for some reason cannot support all the classes moving online, consider using Google Classroom. Google Classroom is a simple yet powerful and free LMS that allows instructors to set up a class in less than a minute. Additionally, it integrates with Google's wide array of programs, platforms, and services, including Gmail, YouTube, Drive, Hangouts, Stream, and Docs. Not only are these excellent apps in themselves, but most people are already familiar with them. Google has even set up a page with a variety of resources on how to put up a class on Google Classroom. Find out more here: https://teacher-center.withgoogle.com/first-day-trainings/welcome-to-classroom.

## Make sure to interact

Online learning presents the option of a live or recorded lecture. While online courses are often asynchronous, the time required to make asynchronous content makes that option prohibitive. But there is also an opportunity here for live interaction with online students who, unlike in traditional online courses, signed up for the course knowing that they needed to be available during a given time slot. Plus, you can record your live broadcasts for anyone who misses them or for future use.

Interactivity will be critical as content alone is rarely rich enough to keep an audience's attention. Thus, it is a good idea to pause every five to 10 minutes for an interaction. Breaking up a lecture is also critical for retention because people sporadically need pauses to engage new information to move it from their working memory to their long-term memory. You can also intersperse these interactions with videos. Thus, try talking for five minutes, showing a video, talking for another five minutes, doing an interaction, and so on.

A simple interaction is to ask the class a question and solicit answers either via the chat function in video conferencing software or by audio. Just make sure to tell students to mute themselves when they are not speaking to avoid a cacophony of noises. A better option, however, is to use an audience response system to prime the pump with questions that invite responses from all students at the same time. Poll Everywhere (https://www.polleverywhere.com/) allows you to incorporate polls into PowerPoint slides so that you do not need to change systems to run it. Kahoot! (https://kahoot.com/) is a more feature-rich system, but if you are using a PowerPoint you will need to switch back and forth between applications to run it. This is where having dual monitors or running two computers at once is helpful as the audience response system will be running outside of the video conferencing system. Have the audience response system running on the other computer or monitor and set up the questions ahead of time. Then swing over to activate a question and have students answer on their smartphones.

Real or hypothetical scenarios are ideal for opinion questions. Here is one I use in my medical ethics class:

> An elderly man needs a kidney transplant, and his daughter is tested for a match. As his care provider you find out that she is not a match because she is not actually his daughter. Do you tell the man that she is not his daughter? Do you tell the daughter?

After presenting your prompt, you might start by asking students submit a simple yes or no to gauge where they stand. Make sure to screencast the results. People love watching the graph columns move around as responses come in, and this will get students interested in defending their positions. Then you can open the question up to discussion, either verbally or in the chat.

For factual topics, you might ask a multiple-choice question and, after the responses are recorded, give the correct answer. That will not only indicate how well students understood the material and whether you need to go over it again but also get students who submit the wrong answer vested in finding out why they got it wrong.

Another option is to give the students a question and ask who can get the right answer first. Students are generally more willing to venture a guess in an online chat than live because of the embarrassment of getting something wrong in front of others. This may come as a surprise for faculty who feel like getting students to talk live can be like pulling teeth.

**Looking ahead**

I have long argued that online education allows for continuity in higher education, but it requires preparation. Ideally, institutions would create an LMS companion to every course, face-to-face or otherwise. The companion would at the very least host all course resources and assessments. But putting lecture content online as well would not only make the companion a complete plug-and-play backup but also allow students who miss class to get course content.

Remember that real online teaching is not simply recording yourself lecture. Doing so doesn't take advantage of the web as its own communication medium. If you are new to online teaching, take this opportunity to learn more about how real online courses are created and consider how your lectures might be converted into rich, educational online content as part of a course companion in the future.

# Keep Calm and Redesign with Perspective

*Bridget Arend*

Sometimes we are asked to step during an emergency situation when a colleague cannot finish teaching a course. Sometimes enrollment or structural changes mean we are unexpectedly assigned to take on a new course just days before the semester starts. And sometimes, beyond our wildest imaginations, a pandemic causes us to reformat our on-campus courses for online delivery overnight.

All these options are far from ideal. As someone who regularly helps faculty thoughtfully redesign their courses, I know that quality course design takes time. Ideally, we want any redesign process to involve rethinking assumptions, developing a clear sense of overall goals, considering internal and external expectations, and tinkering (sometimes excessively) with content, resources, assignments, and instructional activities. A thorough course redesign is best completed when you have carved out some time and space for fresh thinking. But what do we do without the luxury of time?

If you're currently teaching a course that needs to be retooled, restructured, or redesigned midstream, here are a few things to keep your expectations realistic and your sanity intact.

### Focus on long-term goals

In an unexpected course redesign situation, many questions are going to emerge before you have the time to think them through. Can students complete alternative assignments? What if a student misses an essential component of the course? What if your final exam or class presentations need to occur online? At this point we can borrow some lessons from the established course design models, such as integrated course design (Fink, 2013) and backward design processes (Wiggins & McTighe, 2011). It is immensely valuable to have a clear mental picture of our end goal.

While we may be tempted to start planning what needs to happen tomorrow, taking even just 20 minutes to breathe, step back, and write out the long-term goals for student learning can help us make the right decisions in the short term. What do you hope that students will carry with them long after completing this course? What impact do you want this course—or the current situation—to have on their lives? These are not small questions, but the clearer our intentions and purposes are from the outset, the easier it will be to make those "in the moment" decisions.

### Remember that less is more

The benefits of "depth over breadth" approaches to teaching provide value for any course but are especially important when the time frame changes. We may have to face the reality that we simply cannot do everything we want to do in the course and that trying to "get it all in" may actually do more harm than good. Instead, take solace in the value of going deeper in learning—perhaps less reading, less content, and more focus on connections, reflection, and application. Carefully consider what is essential to accomplishing those long-term goals, what could be left out, and ultimately where you want your students to focus their limited time and energy.

### Involve the students

Students can be incredibly supportive and understanding when given the chance. If they know you are doing your best and have their long-term interests at heart, they are often very willing to work with you. Share your long-term goals with them and discuss your planned changes. What if they tried to write the course learning outcomes, in their own words and in ways that make sense given their situations, or even create their own learning plans? Discuss why what they learn in this class matters—or better yet, ask them to make this connection themselves. Why not ask for their suggestions at how best to achieve the learning goals? They may uncover some creative options or find their own technology solutions. You don't have to adopt every idea, but they may come up with some great options, and you'll gain valuable student buy-in through the process.

### Give yourself a break

These are far from ideal situations, and no one can expect perfection. We may even make mistakes—add in too many activities, focus on the wrong resources, or set up a new project that fails. These are mistakes to learn from! Yes, if we had more time, we could do some truly wonderful things. But we can also appreciate the small steps we've taken to support meaningful learning. Be patient, and be kind and gracious to yourself and your students. Keep your eyes on those long-term goals, and celebrate small achievements along the way!

**References**

Fink, L. D. (2013). *Creating significant learning experiences: An integrated approach to designing college courses* (2nd ed.). John Wiley & Sons.

Wiggins, G. P., & McTighe, J. (2011). T*he understanding by design guide to creating high-quality units.* ASCD.

# Simple Tips for Engaging Students in Zoom

*Linda M. Boland and Claire Howell Major*

Prior to the COVID-19 pandemic, relatively few instructors had used web-based conferencing for teaching and learning. With the shift in the spring of 2020, many instructors suddenly found themselves teaching online courses, and many others found themselves teaching onsite with some students using videoconferencing to attend remotely. Having used videoconferencing for both fully online and mixed-format courses ourselves, we have found several ways to use videoconferencing tools, such as Zoom, to promote student engagement and inclusive teaching. Our approaches are flexible enough to accommodate small and large classes and a variety of educational levels and disciplines.

**1. Greet each student by name as they enter the Zoom space.**
- Say their names to give you a chance to welcome them and to allow you to check whether they can hear and see you and vice versa. It's a built-in sound and image check.
- Consider opening up the room for some social interaction before class starts (~10 minutes before class time) and encourage students to chat with each other. This approach simulates the informal atmosphere of walking into class and getting ready for classwork.

**2. Begin with an activity.**
- Get students thinking and set the tone for participation by asking them to do something. This approach serves as a way for students to connect and opens the doors to more interaction as the class continues.
- You can approach this activity in many different ways. For example, you might use a short question and ask students to respond in the

chat or ask them a question on a poll. Or you might start with small groups in breakout rooms and give the students a question to work on together.

**3. Break up any lectures with short questions or polls (this applies to other modes of teaching too, but it is critical to online engagement).**

- About every 10–15 minutes, add a poll or a question in the chat or ask students for an emoji or a thumbs up to vote on something to engage them. This approach helps to focus attention; human attention span, especially on Zoom, is limited.
- Don't just tell them, but explain something and then ask students to solve a problem, make a prediction, or identify a difference between two concepts or approaches. You could also work a sample or show them a strategy and then ask them to use it. Another approach is to prompt them with an image or graph and ask a question about it.

**4. Have a strategy for calling on students and explain it to students; if you change your process mid-course, explain that too.**

- If you intend to call on students to answer questions, plan for how to do this inclusively, and also allow processing time. Ask them to write answers on paper before sharing verbally or in the chat. This approach provides students with time to compose their thoughts and to give better responses.
- To further enhance their thinking time, when you ask them to type in the chat box, also ask them to *not* hit "enter" until you ask everyone to do so. That way, each student can type without interference from the other responses and then everyone will see all of the responses at once when you ask them to hit enter at the same time ("one, two, three, go").
- Note that the chat function shows the students' names with their comments. If you want responses to be anonymous—for example, if you are discussing a delicate topic or want authentic challenge—then consider using something that allows them to submit anonymous responses, such as a Google Doc, Jamboard (https://jamboard.google.com), or Padlet (https://padlet.com/) activity.

**5. Have a strategy for students to ask questions of you or their classmates.**

- Explain to students how you want them to signal that they have a question for you. Providing them direction helps reduce confusion and can actually encourage more questions by eliminating a barrier to participation.

- Consider using the nonverbal feedback tools in Zoom, the chat, or verbal responses when unmuted.
- If you find it distracting to look for hands raised, then consider a rotating role in which a student can help you identify who has a question so that you can call on them to engage with you and the class. If you miss seeing their hand raised, they may not persist, and you will have missed an opportunity to clarify their understanding.
- Consider a way to let students ask questions anonymously or tell them to message you questions privately in the chat; this approach allows students to ask questions without fearing embarrassment.
- Ask students to evaluate how student involvement is working from time to time, and adjust your approach if they offer suggestions that may help them engage to ask and answer questions.

### 6. Be intentional about the size of any breakout rooms.

- Set a specific size for the breakout room, and determine that with intentionality in advance. Breakout rooms can be unwieldy when too many people are in a group. Keeping the size small can help to ensure engagement and participation.
- Typically, you'll want a breakout room of no more than five students.
- Consider breakout rooms of two students only for a think-pair-share type of activity.

### 7. Provide a specific task, a time frame for the task, and a plan for reporting out to the larger group whenever you use breakout rooms.

- Use breakouts with care and make sure you have a good reason or learning goal for using them. You can eliminate common problems with breakout rooms, including that students in the breakout room sometimes don't know exactly what they should be doing or what product is expected of them and that they don't have enough time for complex tasks.
- Let students know if you plan to join any of the breakout room sessions and what you will be doing when you join; also convey whether students can ask you to join their room if they have questions.
- Remember that breakout room tasks seem to take more time than if students were working together at a shared table in a classroom. If the task has multiple parts, break them down in order of priority or consider whether different rooms can take different parts and share

them (like a modified jigsaw activity). Make sure students have the question or task in writing (in the chat or in a collaborative document or your slides).

- Plan for additional time to comment and respond. You can also respond at the start of the next class.
- Ask the students to produce a summary (use the chat or Google Doc or Jamboard for a version of the "minute paper").
- Give each breakout room a two-minute warning when the time is up.
- Don't place breakout sessions at the end of class, since doing so will mean more students are likely to leave; explain that the activity will be brief and let them know how it will fit into what you are doing for the remainder of the session.

## 8. Embrace pauses.

- Use pauses to good effect; they are inevitable in videoconferencing sessions. There will be pauses between questions asked and the answers. There will also be pauses for fully embracing the technology. For example, you will need time to share your screen and students need time to open files you share or navigate to collaborative documents. Slow or unreliable internet connections may also cause delays or interruptions.
- Embrace the pauses rather than displaying frustration about them. Students will benefit from your positivity and your confidence. Moreover, pauses can be beneficial to learning as they offer students time to process.

## 9. Select "record" at the start of the session *if* you plan to record.

- There are good reasons to record class sessions; indeed some institutions require it so that students who were not able to attend can watch the session later. There are also good reasons to not record, as it can be intimidating or challenging for students in a number of ways. Make sure that it is essential to do so before choosing this option, and always be sure to let students know that you are recording if you choose to do so.
- Note that if you are discussing sensitive topics or topics that may be censored in a remote student's country, consider alternative methods. Reach out to your teaching center or faculty colleagues for consultation.

How teachers and students use videoconferencing software for teaching and learning will likely drive future technological improvements. In the meantime, educators can apply creative adaptations to use current technology in ways that promote student engagement even in the absence of a physical classroom.

**More information on using Zoom in your teaching:**
- Breakout rooms: https://support.zoom.us/hc/en-us/articles/206476093-Getting-Started-with-Breakout-Rooms
- Chat: https://support.zoom.us/hc/en-us/articles/203650445-In-Meeting-Chat
- Nonverbal feedback: https://support.zoom.us/hc/en-us/articles/115001286183-Nonverbal-Feedback-During-Meetings
- Polling: https://support.zoom.us/hc/en-us/articles/213756303-Polling-for-Meetings
- Recording Zoom sessions: https://support.zoom.us/hc/en-us/sections/200208179-Recording
- Screen sharing: https://support.zoom.us/hc/en-us/articles/201362153-How-Do-I-Share-My-Screen-

Visit this link to download these tips as a handout:
https://www.teachingprofessor.com/wp-content/uploads/2021/03/Boland-and-Major_SimpleTips_Engaging-in-Zoom_handout-download.docx

# Developing the Professor-Student-Student Bond in Virtual Courses

*David P. Pursell*

When my institution closed because of the pandemic, I was asked to teach an entirely virtual organic chemistry course (class and lab) in the 2020 summer semester. This was the first entirely virtual organic course at our college and my first entirely virtual course of any kind. While one may teach well with technology, Michael Wesch, anthropology professor at Kansas State University, notes that "it doesn't matter what method you use if you do not first focus on one intangible factor: the bond between professor and student" (Young, 2012). I elected to use the flipped classroom approach as I do in face-to-face courses. But my challenge in the virtual environment was to develop the professor-student-student bond, which is essential for a collaborative, team-oriented problem-solving mentality when students and the professor do not have shared face-to-face interactions. I implemented three distinct activities in my virtual course to address the challenge. While the activities were used in organic chemistry, they are adaptable to virtually any course.

## Activity 1: Organic coffee calls with professor

This activity is designed to enhance the professor-student bond. Each student conducts two coffee call meeting activities with me and both are graded events. The first is a 15-minute individual student meeting (Zoom, FaceTime, etc.) with me and touted as low-key, casual, and not about chemistry. We get to know each other and discuss academic, professional, and personal topics to build the professor–student bond. We also address expectations, challenges, and how to be successful in organic chemistry. The first meeting counts for 1 percent of the overall course grade. The second is a similar 15-minute individual student meeting near the end of the semester, counts for 3 percent of the overall course grade, and focuses on a big-picture discussion of the chemistry the student has learned during the course. It is not a gotcha discussion but one designed to draw out from the student that they have actually learned organic chemistry and can articulate their new-found knowledge in a professional-toned conversation. I don't describe it as such, but one might view the second meeting as an end-of-course oral exam of relatively small consequence.

**Activity 2: In-class graded boards**

This activity uses the shared course virtual whiteboard and aims to develop the professor-student-student bond to build collaborative problem-solving capability. To facilitate progress on the board problems, I assign four students to a team and each team has a specific day in the schedule for which they lead the in-class graded boards (ICGBs) for their classmates. I assign each student to two teams of differing student composition during the semester, and the two graded ICGB sessions count for a total of 4 percent of the overall course grade. Teams work together to prepare for their ICGB sessions under my guidance and outside of the synchronous class period, developing collaborative, team-building experiences that nurture the trust, confidence, and knowledge awareness required of successful professionals. During the synchronous class period, the team introduces the assigned problems to classmates, presents problem solutions, answers questions from me and their classmates, and leads discussion.

**Activity 3: Lab teams**

This activity is designed to enhance the student-student bond by assigning students to lab teams of four. The team concept could work equally well for group projects that are not lab-based. In the face-to-face course, students work in pairs to conduct experimental procedures, gather, discuss, and analyze data and then each student writes an individual lab report. For the virtual lab, by contrast, students conduct synchronous and asynchronous experiments with assigned team members. Each member then writes and submits an individual report with input from their team members. I then select one report at random from the team for grading, and every team member receives the same grade from the selected report. Lab reports are worth 21 percent of the overall course grade. New team composition for each of the labs ensures that students have the opportunity to forge bonds with as many classmates as possible. The intent is to incentivize team members to collaborate in completing the virtual experiment and writing the lab report, as the team's grade depends on quality contributions from each member.

**Lessons learned**

I conducted anonymous pre- and post-surveys to gauge student attitudes and to develop lessons learned. For the coffee calls, students were anxious prior to calls, but felt they had developed a personal connection and gained confidence to discuss organic chemistry. Students would like to have a list of topics in advance to prepare for the meetings. For ICGBs students report that it is a very effective activity for building teamwork among the four-student group and with the professor. Students not part of the team, but participating in the synchronous virtual class, felt that the student teams leading problem-solving sessions were more engaging and effective than if I had led the sessions. Students would have liked multiple teams scheduled for each ICGB session to expand participation while tightening the course content for which each team was responsible. Students disliked the lab teams (group projects if not a lab course) concept. Students reported that teams were valuable in helping them develop soft skills while working with classmates but the team lab report grade caused significant stress, especially when one or more of the members were perceived as not contributing to the team effort. While the face-to-face environment provides ample opportunity to develop the professor-student-student bond, activities such as these in the virtual environment may do so as well.

**Reference**

Young, J. R. (2012, February 12). A tech-happy professor reboots after hearing his teaching advice isn't working. *The Chronicle of Higher Education*. https://www.chronicle.com/article/a-tech-happy-professor-reboots-after-hearing-his-teaching-advice-isnt-working

# What Students Want: A Simple, Navigable LMS Course Design

*Eric Loepp*

One of the most important tools instructors have to help establish a productive remote learning experience is one that we do not always talk about: the learning management system (LMS). We often view the LMS as a digital warehouse for course content and a repository for course grades. It can—and should—be more than this. It can be a vibrant hub of digital classroom activity.

At the end of the spring 2020 term, I surveyed students to ask what components of a course made it successful in a remote learning format (Lederman, 2020). Not surprisingly, instructors were rated most pivotal. The second-highest rated feature? A well-managed LMS.

I also asked students to think about the professor that did the best job leading a course remotely. Roughly one-third of students referenced our LMS (Canvas) in their responses. "The best instructors . . . had a Canvas page that was simplistic in nature and easy to follow," reported one student. Said another: "They had a very organized and easy to understand Canvas page." Numerous other descriptors emerged in response to this question: "well-planned out," "set up very well," and "clearly outlined," among others.

When students were asked to offer advice to faculty about effective teaching strategies in a remote setting, the LMS again featured prominently. "Have your Canvas course laid out in a way where students know exactly what is going on in class," requested one student. Another person agreed: "It's annoying when I'm hunting all across a Canvas page because I can't find what I'm looking for." This individual neatly summarizes the collective student view: "A well-managed, well-crafted, clear and understandable Canvas page can be a godsend when working remote."

It is clear that a well-designed and well-managed online course site is vital to student success. But what does that look like? Two key concepts are central: *simplicity* and *navigability*. By simple, I mean digital course spaces that prioritize essential information and relegate or even discard nonessential content. By navigable, I mean digital course spaces that utilize a consistent structure that clearly elucidates class activities and student responsibilities.

Below I offer an example of what a simple and navigable course may look like. I recommend creating a separate module for each unit in a course, arranging them in chronological order, and populating them with an individual page for each class period or each week within that unit. For example, in my introductory course in American government and politics, I create a welcome module with some preliminary information, followed by a module for our first course unit. The unit comprises five weeks of the semester, and each week has a dedicated page within the module.

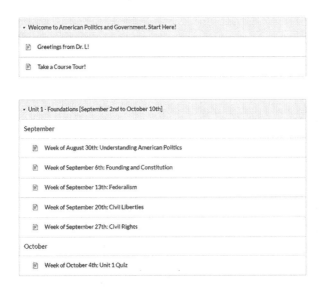

The heart of the course is organized within the weekly pages. These pages should address three key questions: *What should students do before class?*, *What should students do after class?*, and *What are students responsible for delivering this week?* For classes with a remote meeting element, there is a fourth question: *How do I get to class?*

## Week of September 6th: Founding and Constitution

Something to think about: It would be a mistake to think that the debates, arguments, and negotiations that created the federal government are simply artifacts of history. Quite the contrary! While the details and specific issues have changed over time, the same fundamental issues that challenged us then also challenge us now. Perhaps the most basic is this: *what, exactly, should the government be responsible for? In other words, how big should the government be?*

### Step 1: Before Class Meetings To-Do List

- Review textbook chapter two

### Step 2: Join Class Online at 11:00 a.m. on Tuesday and Thursday

- Go to your course calendar, click the tile for the appropriate date, and hit "Join Meeting"

### Step 3: After Class Meetings To-Do List

- Review Supplemental Slide Deck (posted after class) and recording of class (as necessary)
- Here is a neat summary to help differentiate Federalists from Anti-Federalists.
- Review these "Crash Course" videos:
  - On the compromises that led to the Constitution ✎ .
  - On the separation of powers ✎

### Step 4: What Am I Turning In This Week?

- Preliminary Survey
- InQuizitive activity for Chapter 2

*Click "Next" to view our Canvas week on Federalism!*

◂ Previous                                                                 Next ▸

---

I organize these questions into steps within the weekly page. Step 1 provides instructions for what to do before the class meets. Since this example is a remote course that students join virtually, Step 2 describes how to access the class meetings that week. (In my courses that meet face-to-face, Step 2 is simply omitted.)

Step 3 outlines additional activities to complete after our class meetings. For me, this usually includes additional video examples or extra documentation from class to review as necessary. In some cases, such as an upper division research methods course, this step will also include practice problems and answer keys. Finally, Step 4 lists any deliverables students will be submitting that week. Note that active links are embedded as much as possible in order to maximize navigation within the LMS. Reminders about dates and times are also helpful.

To be sure, different courses and instructors have different requirements and preferences, so other instructors may organize things a bit differently. However, the fundamental goals of simplicity and navigability should not vary. Build your pages with these goals in mind. Ask colleagues to review your digital course space with these objectives in mind. Better yet, consult with students before or at the beginning of the semester. We ask for feedback all the time on topics like textbook selection and teaching approach. Why not LMS course design?

Spending time creating simple and navigable LMS courses is extremely worthwhile. In recent years—and especially during the pandemic—colleges and universities have invested considerable energy, time, and money in technological tools to support various modalities of instruction (Grajek, 2020). Equally important should be a commitment to using them *well*. Many pressing concerns in higher education in 2020—such as mental health, emotional health, physical health, and skepticism about online learning quality—will remain prominent concerns for the foreseeable future (Anderson, 2020; The Jed Foundation, 2020; Malani, 2020; OneClass Blog, 2020; Top Hat, 2020).

While LMSs cannot resolve all the challenges we face, they can make a meaningful difference in the academic lives of our students, and perhaps alleviate some of the apprehension our students feel. For instance, a well-designed digital course space can reduce anxiety about finding and completing work. Similarly, for the many students whose familial and work obligations require them to do their classwork at unconventional hours, a simple and navigable course can facilitate learning even if the instructor is not available. One student in my class survey stressed this point by noting that when courses are delivered asynchronously, and "something was confusing, we were not able to raise our hand and clarify" the issue. This lack of clarity may be the difference between submitting an assignment (on time) or not.

The dual goals of simplicity and navigability in digital course design are not valuable *because* of the COVID-19 crisis—the pandemic simply cast their value into clearer relief. I have used variations of the model above for years, although the pandemic certainly prompted me to focus even more acutely on my design goals.

Despite the distressing jolt delivered to higher education in 2020, our collective experience actually underscores a comforting axiom: good teaching practices are good teaching practices. True, some modifications will be necessary under certain circumstances and across disciplines; however, a simple, navigable approach to LMS course design will be valuable long after the COVID-19 pandemic (hopefully) subsides, and students will appreciate it regardless of course modality.

## References

Anderson, G. (2020, September 11). Mental health needs rise with pandemic. *Inside Higher Ed.* https://www.insidehighered.com/news/2020/09/11/students-great-need-mental-health-support-during-pandemic

Grajek, S. (2020, May 15). EDUCAUSE COVID-19 QuickPoll results: Fall planning for education and student support. *EDUCAUSE Review.* https://er.educause.edu/blogs/2020/5/educause-covid-19-quickpoll-results-fall-planning-for-education-and-student-support

The Jed Foundation. (2020, October 22). *Survey of college student mental health in 2020*. https://www.jedfoundation.org/survey-of-college-student-mental-health-in-2020

Lederman, D. (2020, May 20). How college students viewed this spring's remote learning. *Inside Higher Ed*. https://www.insidehighered.com/digital-learning/article/2020/05/20/student-view-springs-shift-remote-learning

Malani, P. N. (2020, August 13). Managing pandemic health risks on college campuses. *The New York Times*. https://www.nytimes.com/2020/08/13/well/family/coronavirus-pandemic-college-campuses-student-health.html

OneClass Blog. (2020, April 1). 75% of college students unhappy with quality of eLearning during Covid-19. *OneClass Blog*. https://oneclass.com/blog/featured/177356-7525-of-college-students-unhappy-with-quality-of-elearning-during-covid-19.en.html

Top Hat. (2020, November 20). *Student sentiment for fall 2020: Survey of 3,412 higher ed students finds educators prioritizing human connections and active learning, influencing higher likelihood of student retention in spring 2021 and beyond* [Press release]. https://tophat.com/press-releases/student-sentiment-for-fall

# Tips for Facilitating Live Online Events

*Sami Lange and Jessica Pardoe (with John Orlando)*

The global pandemic has caused emergency shifts in how we teach. Online learning is nothing new, but transitioning a once-dynamic in-person class to a screen in a synchronous format poses some challenges for "new to synchronous" teaching faculty. As two department chairs at a mid-size community college in California, we found a number of similar themes emerged through our discussions with faculty on how to make the classroom environment transition effectively. Faculty made many of the decisions about curriculum and behavior expectations and attendance in the emergency shift on the fly. The faculty discussions about issues and strategies created a deep conversation about what needs to be included moving forward when thinking about synchronous teaching and how best to present expectations to students up front.

Here we examine the four major topics that faculty need to address to ensure effective synchronous learning environments.

**Privacy**

The question of whether to password protect meetings was decided in favor of password protection by press accounts of Zoom bombing. While the primary concern is disruption by others, a password also allows students to assume that only other students will see them in the conferences. The digital format makes it possible that they will be recorded and their image displayed outside of the class. Instructors should prevent this possibility by turning off the recording option for students as well as by clarifying the policy of not allowing recording of online class sessions.

But what about students' privacy during the event? Should faculty require students to show their faces? On the one hand, students can see each other in face-to-face classes, so a videoconference is not relevantly different in this respect. Plus, many faculty want to ensure that students are fully participating in online events where it is easy to turn on the videoconference and switch to something else.

On the other hand, the video background can reveal parts of a student's personal life that are not on display in their face-to-face classes, such as their bedroom, home, or family. For this reason, some faculty require students to show their faces during the event to ensure participation but allow them to use virtual backgrounds—a function in Zoom and some other video conferencing systems. Students unable to work with virtual backgrounds could put up a blanket or other temporary background. Another option is to allow students to post photos or themselves or an avatar, but use frequent interactions, such as questions and polling, to ensure attention. These frequent interactions are a good idea anyway to improve learning and retention.

Whatever decision you make, clearly state your expectations up front. Include a section in your syllabus labeled "class time" and information about how students should present themselves and what should be behind them.

**Technology etiquette**

It's a good idea to email students the week prior to the start of the course and offer a tech-check as part of the first class (or a pre-class). Offering this option early and doing mic and audio checks are critical to synchronous classrooms that need student participation, such as in breakout rooms during class or for student presentations.

In any videoconference with a sufficiently large group, at least one person will leave their microphone on, broadcasting background noise. Worse yet is when people don't realize that if they type on a laptop keyboard, the vibrations will travel through the casing and shake the highly sensitive mic, making it sound to others like someone is playing the bongos. For these reasons it is important to instruct people to mute themselves until they speak. Students should opt for the use of a desktop, if available, as these computers produce better sound and are not known to have the same feedback loop issues that laptops have. Many students have access only to laptops, including those borrowed from their institutions, however, so instructors should expect to work with the equipment students have.

**Behavior expectations**

Sleeping, eating, and lying down while on screen in the virtual classroom were frequent student behaviors that instructors reported. We do not allow these in face-to-face courses, because they are disrespectful to the speaker and distracting to other students, and for this reason faculty can forbid the behavior in videoconferences. Students need to know what is permissible from the outset. After all, they are learning from the comforts of their own homes with greater opportunities for distraction, and it may be unclear that the expectations of your virtual classroom mirror those of your physical classroom.

Students often do not realize how their behavior might distract others in a videoconference, and so it is a good idea to tell students not to engage in activities that will be of interest to and thus distract others. For instance, a student playing with their cat will elicit the attention of participants while the instructor or a student is speaking and so should not be allowed. "Don't do what you would not do in the face-to-face classroom" is probably a good rule to establish at the beginning of a videoconference within reason. We too are all in extreme circumstances, and some level of compassion and flexibility, within reason, will need to be accepted. It is hard to prevent animals from coming into a room during a videoconference, but students should know not to bring those distractions into the videoconference. Guidelines need to be set, and students also need to know that if their dog barks in the class, it will be OK.

## Live communication strategies

All major videoconferencing systems come with chat, which can be a double-edged sword. The backchannel consists of the private conversations between audience members happening by whisper, text, or Twitter during a live talk, and there have been some examples of speakers broadcasting this backchannel during their talks by giving the audience a chatroom that was projected live during the event on the auditorium screen. The idea was to broaden the range of discussion by giving all audience members access to the thoughts that were previously shared among only a few people.

But this practice faded away when people realized that the backchannel splits people's attention and causes them to miss the talk. Similarly, faculty need to determine how students will use chat during their events. Students are used to communicating by chat, and so allowing an open use of chat will very likely generate more questions. But at the same time chat splits participants' attention such that they will likely miss material. In particular, it is very hard for a speaker to both talk and read chat at the same time. If questions are asked during chat, the speaker is not likely to see them until later, and so there should be no expectation that questions or anything else posted to chat will get an immediate response.

For an American Sign Language course at our institution, a heavily visual course with no audio, the chat feature in Zoom was not allowed at all due to the already high level of visual concentration needed. But for other courses that had teaching assistants, chat was the preferred method of questions because the teaching assistants could monitor and respond to chat without disrupting the presentation.

One thing faculty firmly agreed on was that students interrupting with questions at random times was not preferred. One option is to require students to use the "raise hand" function to ask any questions and to stop the presentation every few minutes to read and respond to questions. These pauses also allow the instructor to read the chat messages and amplify any of them to initiate a new discussion, aiding in additional time for student reflection and retention.

Overall, think about the online classroom as you would in-person courses. How will you communicate best with your students with the virtual tools at your disposal?

# Google Hangouts, Meet, and Duo as Alternatives to Zoom

*John Orlando*

Zoom has become ubiquitous during the COVID-19 crisis to the point of even becoming the butt of a *Saturday Night Live* skit (NBC, April 11, 2020). But while it replaced the equally ubiquitous GoToMeeting seemingly overnight as the go-to app for hosting meetings, it is not without its faults. For one, the 40-minute limit on free accounts has caught many a host by surprise. (My wife and I have twice had our at-home X-Fit class cut out in the middle of a burpee set.) Also, Zoom bombing—intruders invading a Zoom meeting to disrupt it—has gotten a lot of press lately.

But people forget that there are alternatives to Zoom. In particular, Google Hangouts, Meet, and Duo all offer videoconferencing without cost. Each app is designed for a particular type of meeting, and by integrating seamlessly with Google's other apps—such as Drive, Gmail, and YouTube—these systems provide many advantages over Zoom. Here I examine the features and best ways to use each.

## Google Hangouts

Hangouts was released in 2013 as an alternative to GoToMeeting. It was free, easy to open and invite people into, and video focused. While GoToMeeting was built on the assumption that the main window would display the presenter's PowerPoint, Hangouts was designed to allow participants' webcam feeds to fill the main window. In this way GoToMeeting was designed to broadcast one person's presentation to essentially passive viewers, whereas Hangouts meetings felt more like a gathering of equals around a conference table.

While my workgroup instantly started using Hangouts for our

meetings, soon Zoom came along designed on similar a "video first" mode, and many people forgot about Hangouts. But Hangouts offers some advantages over Zoom. For one, its lower profile makes it a less likely target of intruders. Also, it allows for meetings up to 24 hours in length. It works on either a browser or an app and requires only a Google account to set up a meeting. Plus, it is built to stream YouTube videos without causing stalling problems on the user's end because videos stream directly from YouTube to the users without having to go through the presenter's computer.

Keep in mind that Hangouts has a 10-participant limit on its free plan. But if your institution is accredited and not-for-profit, it can sign up for G Suite for Education for free. This allows all faculty, staff, and students to have access to the myriad of apps in the Google constellation at the premium level. For instance, the Hangouts participant limit goes up to 25 with G Suite. Many K–12 school districts as well as some higher education institutions have switched to G Suite and are very happy with it, and so it is well worth lobbying your institution to sign up for this free service.

These advantages and limitations make Hangouts good for small group conversations, such as live meetings between students for group projects. The G Suite limit of 25 might also makes it work for a class-wide meeting, depending on the size of your class. Finally, you can record Hangouts with its free version, which makes it good for recording screencasts, thought the process is a bit convoluted. Zoom's free version does not allow recording. You can get started with Hangouts here: https://hangouts.google.com/.

**Google Meet**

Google Hangouts recently spawned two new apps called Meet and Duo. Meet is designed for larger meetings of up to 100 participants. It even allows for up to 250 participants and 100,000 viewers in live stream. Until now, Meet has required a G Suite subscription to use, but Google just made Meet free to anyone with a Google account until September 30, 2020. It normally has a 60-minute time limit, though Google is also waiving this until at least September 30.

Meet has more features than Hangout and is comparable to Zoom in most regards. One nice advantage over Zoom is that users can send files through the chat feature, which is curiously missing from Zoom. There are many times when I wished I could share a file in Zoom, so this is a big plus for me—and I'm sure for others as well. Meet also allows for email integration with both Gmail and Outlook, while Zoom integrates only with Outlook. Plus, call in is included with Meet, whereas it requires an upgrade in Zoom. Finally, there is no add-on required to use Meet; Zoom requires an add-on.

Teachers who use Meet are very positive about it. The size limit makes it ideal for class-wide meetings and the live stream function is a great way to broadcast events to the public, such as a department or school talk. Like Zoom, you get a specific meeting ID that can be reused, which is very convenient for repeated meetings. The only real knock on Meet is that it relegates the controls and default user feeds to a box underneath the main screen, which some people find a bit messier than the more integrated look of Zoom. I happen to like the setup because I often find myself needing to move the video feed bar around my Zoom screen to keep it from covering up content, but others prefer the Zoom design. Learn more about Meet here: https://blog.google/products/meet/bringing-google-meet-to-more-people.

**Google Duo**

Google Duo is a lesser-known app that is gaining popularity by the minute. It is designed to compete with Skype and FaceTime by facilitating one-on-one conversations between individuals and small meetings of up to 12 people. You can quickly start a voice or video conversation with someone by using their phone number or email address from your contacts, similar to making a phone call. This makes Meet particularly good for phone conferences on the run, though it can also be used on a computer.

Duo comes with a couple of features that make it an attractive alternative to competing apps. One, you can leave a video message for someone who does not answer a call. Two, its Knock Knock feature shows the video of the person calling to the person receiving the call before they answer. This allows the receiver to filter out unwanted calls. Learn more about Duo here: https://duo.google.com/about.

Notice how Duo and Meet occupy opposite ends of the videoconferencing spectrum, with Duo working better for small meetings and Meet working better for large ones. Duo is ideal for quick conversations and help sessions with individual students—essentially, for virtual office hours. Hangouts occupies a middle ground that overlaps the two other apps, leading some to believe that it might be phased out in the future. Between these apps you get viable alternatives to Zoom with specific functionality designed for different uses and audiences.

**Reference**
Dillet, R. (2020, April 2). Zoom freezes feature development to fix security and privacy issues. https://techcrunch.com/2020/04/02/zoom-freezes-feature-development-to-fix-security-and-privacy-issues

# App Smashing for Virtual Presentations

*Madeline Craig*

With the pandemic came a flurry of faculty quickly moving their courses online. The question I heard most during this time was, How can I move my students' presentations online? Most faculty chose to have students do live video presentations with a system such as Zoom. But videoconferencing comes with drawbacks. The biggest is that all students must be present at once, which can be a problem in online courses that some students chose because their schedules make it hard to meet at regularly scheduled class times. Also, technical problems with bandwidth and the like often intrude on these videoconferences.

An alternative format is asynchronous presentations. Students create the presentation, add their voice narration, record it, and post it online for other students to watch and comment on. An advantage is that students can watch the presentation whenever they have the time. Plus, they can post comments and questions on the presentation after thinking about it—an improvement on live presentations, during which they may not think of questions in time to ask them. There is also not as big of a bandwidth issue, because not everyone is online at once.

Asynchronous presentations require two things: a system for recording the presentation and a system for hosting the result online. While students tend to default to PowerPoint for making presentations, I prefer Buncee, an online presentation tool (https://app.edu.buncee.com/). When using Buncee, students can choose from 2,000 existing templates, or they can start with a blank page and add features such as text, shapes, animations, stickers, messages, emoji, web images, 360 images, YouTube videos, and uploads of your own documents, videos, or images. In addition, Buncee has a drawing feature and users can add free response questions and multiple-choice questions to a page for engagement. The other distinguishing feature is the ability to record up to three minutes of video on each page. Buncee offers both a free and paid option so students can create without buying an account.

Although there are many ways to have students present online, I suggest *app smashing* Buncee and Flipgrid. In the simplest terms, app smashing means to combine more than one technology. The combination of Buncee and Flipgrid was perfect for my teacher candidates. Flipgrid, at its most basic level, is a video discussion tool. I have my students use Buncee to create and record their presentations and then use Flipgrid to share and comment on each other's. It is a somewhat simple app smash that works well to not only engage students in the course content but also assess their learning. This app smash is based on effective elements of an educational experience: social, cognitive, and teaching presence (Garrison et al., 1999). Including opportunities for interactions between faculty and students, students and content, and students and other students is accomplished in this virtual presentation method.

First, I ask students to create a presentation using Buncee. Presentations could be created in a more typical presentation tool, such as Google Slides or PowerPoint, and this app smash would work similarly. I like Buncee because I teach future teachers, and Buncee is a dynamic creation tool that includes a wide variety of templates my students might use in future lesson plans. For my assignment, students had to tell the story of their research project using all the features in Buncee, including animations, stickers, backgrounds, uploads (video and images), and text. I then directed them to record themselves presenting the content. Buncee has a built-in recording function, so students open their webcams and record themselves presenting each slide. If you decide to use Google Slides or PowerPoint, students can use the built-in recording features available in these tools. Students could screen record using Screencast-O-Matic, which provides up to 15 minutes of free screen recording.

Once students created and recorded their presentations, it was time for a learning exchange using Flipgrid. I directed students to a designated discussion in Flipgrid to record a video of themselves introducing their research topic and asking their classmates a question about their presentation. I integrate Flipgrid into my school's learning management system, Canvas, to make the grading easier, but you could also provide a link or join code and direct students to flipgrid.com. At the end of the recording, just before they submit their video to the discussion, Flipgrid gives students the option to add a link. Once each student added their video and link to the Flipgrid discussion, their classmates were able to hear their video introduction and the question they needed to answer in their response. Then they viewed their classmates' recorded presentations by clicking the link posted just below that video in Flipgrid. Lastly, each student replied in their own recorded video, answering their classmate's question about the presentation. I encouraged all students to go back to the discussion, watch my reply and their classmates' replies, and reflect on the answers and feedback.

Students really seemed to like using Buncee's features to tell the story of their research projects. During the isolated time of COVID-19, they felt more connected by being able to watch each other present their topics and share their thoughts and feedback through Flipgrid videos. I wrote each step of this process out for students in Canvas, and I provided detailed video instructions using Flipgrid shorts videos embedded in the Canvas assignment. So what did students think of this app smash last semester? Here are some comments from my self-initiated, end-of-semester Google Form:

- "I think Buncee in general is a great program to use, and it was interesting to get to see everyone explain their own presentations without any pressure."
- "I like the Buncee presentation because you get comfortable presenting through video."
- "I enjoy doing presentations and liked using Buncee and thought recording was fun."
- "Responding through Flipgrid . . . is a great way to learn who your classmates are."
- "I think keep the recording of the research presentations! It gives a feel that we are in the classroom when someone else is presenting. Rather than having to read 15 different papers, we were able to hear them from our classmates."
- "I really enjoyed the Buncee project and I enjoyed the videos you included as instructions."
- "I really enjoyed the use of Flipgrid throughout this course especially because we were remote. I enjoyed going back to watch my classmates responses to my Buncee presentation and hearing their feedback!"

**STEPS FOR APP SMASHING:**
**Recorded presentation + Flipgrid video discussion = student learning and engagement**

1. *Create presentation.*
2. *Narrate presentation.*
3. *Record presentation using Buncee or another video-recording app.*
4. *Record a Flipgrid video introduction to your topic with a question to your classmates, and be sure to add the presentation link to your video submission in Flipgrid.*
5. *Watch your classmates' video introductions and their recorded presentations by clicking the link in their Flipgrid video.*
6. *Reply in a Flipgrid video to your classmates' questions.*
7. *Return to Flipgrid to watch your classmates' and instructor's responses to the question you posed about your topic.*

**Reference**

Garrison, D. R., Anderson, T., & Archer, W. (1999). Critical inquiry in a text-based environment: Computer conferencing in higher education. *The Internet and Higher Education, 2*(2–3), 87–105. https://doi.org/10.1016/S1096-7516(00)00016-6

# Universally Designing in Universal Chaos

*Lauren Tucker*

As we all experienced, 2020 turned higher education on its head while spinning and trying to solve a Rubik's Cube. I was lucky enough to have experience with online teaching and hybrid teaching, but my personal turmoil and childcare challenges resulted in sheer panic at the upcoming semester. Having a background in special education, I was always an advocate for Universal Design for Learning (UDL). Planning our courses to be accessible to any student that might enroll can improve the learning experience for all students, especially those with learning challenges. I lived UDL by choice before 2020, now I *need* UDL to survive . . . and so do my students.

UDL focuses on proactively embedding multiple opportunities for students to learn material, engage with the course, and express their learning (CAST, 2020). Keeping UDL at the forefront of my course design during the pandemic has provided much needed stability and consistency within my courses. I keep the following three guidelines in my course planning, and I have seen significant benefits within my courses.

## 1. Remaining predictable and true to myself

Student engagement can be a significant challenge in online courses, especially for students who didn't sign up for a program with fully online courses (all of mine!). At the beginning of the semester, establishing a clear routine within a course can be hugely beneficial, especially in this time of uncertainty. I create weekly course plans (Boettcher & Conrad, 2016) sent through our learning management system with specific expectations for the week. My goal is to keep the course expectations and requirements organized for students (and myself). Another priority is to keep my personality, teaching style, and passion alive in a fully online format. One of the ways my personality permeates my course is through the weekly announcements.

On the day of our class, I submit an announcement with explicit instructions on how we are meeting (asynchronous or synchronous), topics covered for the week, and assignment expectations. This strategy enhances students' ability to manage information and resources, a component of multiple means of representation in the UDL framework (CAST, 2020). The image below includes an example of a weekly announcement. The recipe I use for my announcements is

- a personal message or meme;
- reminder of class meeting method; and
- tasks for the week.

Other people: It's still summer, there's no need to rush into fall

Me:

Happy Wednesday! September is ALMOST over and here we are in Week 5! There is an optional check in for tonight at 7:40pm where I will review the work due for Week 5. I will record and post in the Week 5 folder. I included the link to our class below (also in Course Info):

Join Zoom Meeting

Week 5 Asynchronous Steps for Completion:
Module work due 9/30 --- Case Study due 9/30 (submit in the assignments tab on the left)

**Step 1:**

-Review content in Step 1 and take notes.

-Submit under Step 2 by 9/30/20 by 11:59pm.

**Step 2:**

- Review content on "HLP #13" and take notes.

- Watch classroom example and evaluate the use of accommodations and modifications.

- Submit notes under Step 2 by 9/30/20 by 11:59pm.

These announcements are sent via the learning management platform (we use Blackboard). Students are told at the beginning of the semester that announcements will be used to introduce weekly content. These announcements serve initially as executive functioning supports to organize the weekly topics and tasks for students. Secondarily, they convey my personality to maintain my teaching and social presence within the online course (Garrison et al., 1999).

## 2. Keeping consistency

Consistency in organization and presentation has been indispensable in my online courses. Using the same frame to present the weekly content and activities allows me to focus my student interactions on teaching content vs course navigation challenges. My teaching presence (Garrison & Arbaugh, 2007) is displayed through the systematic directions and steps to engage with the content each week. I use visual cues as multiple means of representation for directional supports within the course. For example, I have a home symbol for the weekly home page and arrow buttons linking to the next step of content. I also use a speaker symbol to remind students they can use a text to speech tool to listen to the text. UDL emphasizes the use of multiple methods to engage with content and to promote understanding (CAST, 2020). Although the activities, resources, and learning goals change each week, the format in which they are presented remains uniform.

This frame also keeps me organized when building my asynchronous classes for students to complete. I use a blank template to add the content each week. The outline below displays an example of my consistent weekly frame added in our learning management system.

- Weekly learning goals
- Recording of me reviewing weekly content
- Specific steps for completion
- Step 1 folder
- Step 2 folder
- Step 3 folder
- Homework for the next class

Using this template allows me to establish system and transparency as I build my online content, which is vital to student navigation (Nilson & Goodson, 2018). At the beginning of the pandemic I found myself clouded by stress and misguided by worry when sitting to develop content, never previously having experienced this in my teaching. The implementation of this framework gives me a clear routine and allows me to ensure my content is focused on student learning and course outcomes, which can be so easily shrouded by "online busywork." To avoid the creation of superficial online work, as I plan each activity, I align it to the course and weekly learning outcomes. This alignment is essential to prioritizing deep engagement with the essential learning material.

## 3. Allowing options

Instilling student choice within my course structure enhances student engagement and their ability to express learning more fluidly (CAST,

2020). Especially during this pandemic, students have frequently expressed the "lack of control" they have felt in their personal and professional lives, which is a common feeling in the midst of a pandemic (Usher et al., 2020). Designing at least one opportunity for individual choice within each asynchronous class has enhanced student engagement and empowerment in courses.

For example, one way I incorporate student choice is during note taking. I use active note taking as a formative assessment to gather evidence on my students' learning process throughout the course (Khan et al., 2017). An emoji is added as a symbol to indicate when students need to respond to a question for submission. In addition to the emoji ☺, I increase ***the size of the question, and it is bolded and italicized.*** I allow students to choose their method of response: typed, handwritten, audio, or video. I have established a video-based discussion board through Flipgrid (http://www.flipgrid.com) for the course, where students can post reflections for any asynchronous notes. Many students have expressed relief that they can handwrite their notes and attach pictures instead of typing. This flexibility relays the message to my students that I value their unique learning preferences as adult learners. Adding in this consideration of "What are my students choosing?" during my design process prioritizes UDL within my course and helps contribute to my student engagement. Student choice also respects the adult learner to establish control in their learning experience, especially when they have been involuntarily forced into online learning.

**In closing**

During these times of uncertainty, having a plan, routine, and controlling what we can is vital. Although we are living (and learning) in unprecedented times, the reality is our students still need to learn and we are expected to facilitate that learning. *How* we design that experience is crucial to positive outcomes. I know each week and activity I plan isn't perfect… heck…some have failed, but that is how I grow. Reflecting on what worked, what didn't, and how to adjust has helped me move forward. Gathering my students' feedback on their learning or aspects of activities that worked helps me to continually improve my course design.

Establishing these design routines grounded in UDL allow for consistency and stability for me and my students. Who knows what new challenges the upcoming semesters will bring, but keeping UDL as a frame to design learning will help my teaching improve and focus on the essentials.

## References

Boettcher, J. V., & Conrad, R. M. (2016). *The online teaching survival guide: Simple and practical pedagogical tips.* John Wiley & Sons.

CAST. (2020). About Universal Design for Learning. https://www.cast.org/impact/universal-design-for-learning-udl

Garrison, D. R., Anderson, T., & Archer, W. (1999). Critical inquiry in a text-based environment: Computer conferencing in higher education. *The Internet and Higher Education, 2*(2–3), 87–105. https://doi.org/10.1016/S1096-7516(00)00016-6

Garrison, D. R., & Arbaugh, J. B. (2007). Researching the community of inquiry framework: Review, issues, and future directions. *The Internet and Higher Education, 10*(3), 157–172. https://doi.org/10.1016/j.iheduc.2007.04.001

Khan, A., Egbue, O., Palkie, B., & Madden, J. (2017). Active learning: Engaging students to maximize learning in an online course. *Electronic Journal of e-Learning, 15*(2), 107–115. https://academic-publishing.org/index.php/ejel/article/view/1824

Nilson, L. B., & Goodson, L. A. (2018). *Online teaching at its best.* Jossey-Bass.

Usher, K., Durkin, J., & Bhullar, N. (2020). The COVID-19 pandemic and mental health impacts. *International Journal of Mental Health Nursing, 29*(3), 315–318. https://doi.org/10.1111/inm.12726

# HyFlex Teaching: An Overview

*John Orlando*

The HyFlex teaching model has drawn considerable attention recently as an alternative to the online, face-to-face, and hybrid teaching models. A HyFlex course is offered both face-to-face and online at once. But instead of dividing course activities between the two modes, as a hybrid course does, a HyFlex course offers all the activities in both modes and allows students to choose which mode they would like to use. Students can even go back and forth between modes during the course. Brian Beatty (2020) notes that there are two ways to implement HyFlex teaching. The first, remote viewing, involves broadcasting the face-to-face session to students not in attendance. In the second, dual tracks, a traditional online course is run simultaneously with a live course. Below I examine both forms of HyFlex, the challenges with each, and how to implement them during the pandemic.

## Remote viewing

Remote viewing is the simplest option as it merely requires placing a camera in the face-to-face course, miking up the teacher, and broadcasting live to YouTube or any of a number of other video-hosting sites. That broadcast can also be recorded for students who could not attend synchronously. I recommend having a dedicated camera operator rather than just leaving a still camera at the back of the room; it is very hard to maintain concentration on a small figure walking back and forth in front of a stationary camera. Plus, people may stand up in front of the camera, and the viewer is unlikely to hear anyone asking a question.

But what this method gains in simplicity, it loses in effectiveness. It treats the online viewer as an afterthought and can give them the impression of peeking into the lecture hall from the rafters. The online medium is fundamentally different from the face-to-face one. Nobody wants to watch someone speak in front of a camera for 45–70 minutes, and it will not take long for the viewer to lose attention.

The instructor will also need to find a way to involve online students in in-class activities. If the instructor asks students questions during class, online students could be given a chat room to type in answers. The chat could be visible to the instructor on their computer; they can then repeat the comments to the live audience or, better yet, broadcast them to everyone through an in-class projector. Another option is to have remove students use videoconferencing software, such as Zoom, to both view and comment via video, again broadcast through the in-class projector. That way, if a remote student wants to speak, they can click the hand-raising icon in the video-conferencing system, and the instructor can pick them to speak to the entire class through the projector and speakers. This would help bring the online students into the live class, though it would be tricky for the instructor to juggle in-class and remote commenting at once. But this method would likely require a dedicated technician to manage. In-class quizzing is easier to handle as both online and in-class students can use the same app (e.g., Kahoot!) to answer instructor questions.

Including online students in in-class group activities is a bigger challenge. If an instructor wants to break the class into small groups for discussions, they can put the online students into similar groups using videoconferencing breakout rooms. Again, the institution would need to assign a staff member or perhaps student to set up and manage these rooms as the course is running. It would be easiest to assign the groups and rooms at the beginning of the semester so that students know which room to jump into whenever a group discussion is called, but in a true HyFlex class that allows students to either come to class or watch online, those breakout rooms cannot be assigned ahead of time because it will not be known which students will come or stay home on any given day.

In any case, videoconference group discussions will be preferable to in-class discussions in a situation of social distancing. Assuming that the institution will want to keep students at least six feet apart this fall, there might not be enough space in the classroom to separate students. Even if there is, students will need to speak to each other from a distance, leading to a cacophony of noise. It might be that instructors will need to give up all in-class group activities during the pandemic, though one workaround is to have students text each other from their seats. It might look odd, but students are used to communicating like this.

## Dual tracks

The dual-track model of running a regular online course in tandem with the face-to-face course gives the online students content that is designed for them. A typical in-class lecture can be converted into short videos in the digital storytelling style of narration with images, graphics, animation, and the like. The instructor can put questions after each video to help with retention or incorporate them right into the videos using systems such as EdPuzzle.

Not only does the dual-track option provide the online students with better learning content, but it also gives them the option of choosing the mode that works best for them—the underlying goal of the HyFlex model. The online students who view videos can rewatch parts they missed or did not understand the first time. But other students might need the structure of having to be in class at a designated time to avoid missing classes. Some students might even want to do both. Those with jobs or sports conflicts on particular days can do the online version of the class then, and students who attended the in-class version might go home and go through the material again online if they believe they missed important points in the live class. Perhaps having the same material delivered by different modalities will help it click for many students.

The big drawback of the dual-track model is that it means more work for the instructor. An instructor who needs to monitor both the face-to-face and online versions of the class may end up doing twice as much work. Plus, if students are allowed to choose their mode on a day-to-day basis, the instructor will need to keep the two tracks in sync. Instructors often fall short of covering all the material they expected to cover in a given class and catch up in the next class or just skip it. But then some students may not get the same content as others, creating a problem for assessments.

While the HyFlex model has been looked at as a response to COVID-19, it does not work in its pure form of allowing day-to-day choice because of the need to split up the class for social distancing. Institutions cannot assume that on any given day no more than the maximum number of students needed for social distancing will show up, and so instructors will need to assign students to one mode or the other at the beginning of the semester.

Despite these issues, the HyFlex model holds promise as a means of better serving the needs of all learners, and I do not doubt that it will become more popular in the coming years as the distinction between traditional, full-time, on-campus students and working adult, part-time students continues to be blur, making flexibility in learning more valuable.

**Reference**

Lederman, D. (2020, May 13). The HyFlex option for instruction if campuses open this fall. *Inside Higher Ed*. https://www.insidehighered.com/digital-learning/article/2020/05/13/one-option-delivering-instruction-if-campuses-open-fall-hyflex

# Reflecting on Effective Teaching Strategies: Faculty Share Their Successes

*Samantha Clifford*

To help direct students in their learning during the pandemic, we as faculty have been tasked with harnessing a range of digital technologies. Acquiring these additional skills has been easier for some, more challenging for others. Faculty at Northern Arizona University, where I teach, moved to a remote and synchronous teaching environment last fall. Below are student engagement strategies shared by faculty who were able to reflect on their successes with remote teaching. These include engagement strategies for synchronous and asynchronous learning, ideas for managing the class in the synchronous and remote learning environments and ensuring instructor presence.

**Engagement strategies for synchronous sessions**
- "Ask a question and have everyone type their answer in chat BUT NOT HIT ENTER. Then give them a countdown and have everyone hit enter at once. If you download the chat, this can be used to assess participation or attendance in the session."—John Tingerthal, Construction Management
- "Each week I have five students do 'My Favorite Movie.' They present a clip or a trailer, then talk about why they chose the film and give the class a chance to discuss it. This works best when they simply post the link in chat. Very enjoyable and informative."—Paul Helford, Communication
- "A think-pair-share question is asked with a polling tool. Depending

on the results, I decide if the 'pair-share' is necessary. I usually say something like, 'We have a range of answers, so you will work in break out rooms to convince your group.' After a set time, we vote again and hopefully converge on the correct answer. If convergence is not achieved, I will explain why one of the answers is false and then have them discuss again for a minute or so to determine the correct one."—Edwin Anderson, Astronomy and Planetary Science

**Participation ideas for asynchronous learning**

- "Homework questions are answered in a Google Chat room and graded as 'participation.' Students are required to ask at least one question per week either in Chat or the LMS virtual classroom. They self-report how often they participate, but I remind them to be honest because I have the records."—Robin Tuchscherer, Civil Engineering, Construction Management, and Environmental Engineering
- "I hide digital 'Easter eggs' in my materials. For example, in a pre-recorded lecture video I show a random link for a few seconds to a Google form where they can enter their name, get a code, and get extra credit by entering that code into the LMS. I hide a link to another in my syllabus. A few times a semester I drop a link for them into the comments field when grading to see who's actually reading the comments. I call these 'curiosities' because my primary aim is for students to practice being more curious, but on a practical level they also help keep students engaged."—Curtis Smith, Boundaryless
- "Students are placed into breakout rooms in the LMS and then use a link to a shared Google Slide workspace to draw what their education would have looked like if the No Child Left Behind federal mandate was not in place during their K–12 educational experience. They are able to connect the course materials with their personal experience and have an alternative to a text-based group assignment."—Samantha Clifford, Anthropology
- "A guided notes outline is provided to students before class via the LMS. There are missing words and details where students respond, process, or apply concepts while following as they watch the recording of a short lecture. There is a Q and A section (built into the LMS) where these students can post, share, and ask questions; we go over these questions in the synchronous meeting."—Holly Aungst, Health Sciences

## Managing class in the synchronous and remote learning environment

- "Research teams are created at the start of the semester. One person from each team is required to attend in person and log into the LMS virtual classroom as well. The other team members work with the in-person student in break out groups in class. Having someone physically in the class to raise their hand when they have a question makes it easier for them to get my attention and ask questions and hear the (sometimes long) answers."—Lisa Tichavsky, Criminology and Criminal Justice

- "I assign a student as a technology assistant each day. They monitor the chat to let me know if there are questions that I am missing. I found that when all students were remote, I could manage, but as soon as I needed to divide my attention with in-person students, I was missing questions. Students are sheepish about interrupting and tend to ask their questions via chat. Having a student whose job is to interrupt helps me make sure I am not moving on while there are still questions."—Rachel Neville, Math and Statistics

## Ensuring instructor presence

- "I log into Zoom on two different computers at the same time for each of my classes so that the students can see the material from one computer's camera, me from the other computer's camera, and the students in the classroom from the room camera. Multiple students have told me that they really like being able to see me and the material; it helps them to better connect with the class and the content."—Melissa Schonauer, Honors

- "I send a P.S. email that summarizes the day's activities and reiterates assignments. At the end of these emails, I 'invite' students to attend the next class and ask them to RSVP. This also provides them with an opportunity to ask clarifying questions about current subjects we are exploring."—Lawrence Lenhart, English

While all these strategies focus on fostering engagement and maintaining motivation, some of the most powerful endeavors entail reaching out to students who are struggling with the new learning format. As an instructional designer, I am witness to the incredible effort faculty are investing in their intentional preparation, transition to accessible content, and altering their assessments to be more authentic. Students notice and appreciate the effort. Please keep in mind that this effort can serve as a model for work expected in the course, in addition to highlighting your concern for your students' success.

# Trauma-Informed Teaching: During the Transition to Virtualized Learning and in Response to the Coronavirus Pandemic

*Mays Imad and Lisa C. Schumaier*

After the coronavirus pandemic hit the US, our institution quickly moved to virtual learning. As faculty developers and instructors, we felt that the Teaching and Learning Center was set up to effectively mobilize our faculty and staff, offer direct instruction and guidance, and provide everyone with a supportive and safe community. Most colleges had to rush to virtual teaching, with faculty learning multiple new apps, interfaces, and within weeks building a new virtual vernacular and literacy. There is a social and emotional component that was always at risk of being overlooked but was perhaps the most effective at mitigating the more severe effects of such rapid transition.

Recognizing that we are all experiencing the impact and trauma of a global pandemic, we have created a chart that outlines the six principles to a trauma-informed approach as recommended by the Centers for Disease Control and Prevention in conjunction with the National Center for Trauma-Informed Care (https://www.cdc.gov/cpr/infographics/6_principles_trauma_info.htm). This chart (on the following page) contains tips to use while teaching virtually to alleviate the effects of trauma as well as build resilience and self-empowerment so you and your students can heal and thrive.

Many of us are heading into the fall semester heavy-hearted, anxious, or experiencing traumatic stress. The pandemic is not only a physical crisis or an institutional crisis but also a profound emotional crisis. Parker Palmer states, "We teach who we are." Right now, we are heartbroken, uncertain, and stressed, but we are also still full of love and hope for our students and our disciplines. We cannot give what we do not have. We must first pay attention to our own trauma and mitigate its impact on our ability to teach and help our students learn and flourish.

> Visit this link to download a PDF version of the chart:
> https://s26600.pcdn.co/wp-content/uploads/2020/08/Imad-and-Schumaier_Trauma-Informed-Teaching_Chart-4.pdf

| PRINCIPLES | TIPS | REFERENCES |
|---|---|---|
| Principle 1:<br>Ensure emotional, cognitive, physical, and interpersonal **safety** | • First and foremost, consider how *you* are doing. Your safety is equally important, and we encourage you to continue to reach out to colleagues in your department as well as your teaching and learning centers and your counseling department.<br>• Continue to communicate with your students. Communicate not only for the sake of communicating but also to remind students that you are a constant—that you are here for them and want them here too. Let them know they are not alone.<br>• Continue to address students using their names. Ask them how they are doing. This will reinforce to them that you "see" them and they matter.<br>• As much as possible, offer multiple modes of communication to reach as many students as possible and encourage interactive engagement.<br>• When possible, share stories about yourself to help your students get to know who they are learning from.<br>• Encourage your students to keep a positive affirmation daily journal. (You might keep one online to model it to your students.) For example, ask your students to simply fill in the blank on the following sentences:<br>  • I am _____.<br>  • I have _____.<br>  • I am looking forward to _____.<br>• Create a Google Doc for your entire class and ask students to share tips for coping with social isolation and what they're grateful for. | Webinar for Faculty: Trauma- Informed Teaching & Learning (https://youtu.be/XqcTbipuFDQ)<br><br>Webinar for Students: Stress, Anxiety, Trauma, & Learning; Emotional Regulation for Better Learning(https://pima.zoom.us/rec/play/75x8cempjjg3HtKcsQSD-C_V-W9XufausgCUar6IKnUu0VSUBZFCjY-bUbY-oEd-hPGMkmWtFOn9nvlhQI)<br><br>Pima's TLC workshop: Writing as a Bridge (https://pima.zoom.us/rec/play/6Jwul-yrjw3EoGd4wSD-BvV-W46-LqOs1Sce8vAKmB61WiUHOwW-mZrZBZbaYIYPyfuF3ClZDWecnMEwq) |

| Principle 2: Foster **trustworthiness** and **transparency** | • Establish early and ongoing communication affirming your continual presence as an instructor.<br>• When possible, share stories about yourself to help your students get to know who they are learning from.<br>• Inform students without inundating them with information they may be too overwhelmed to process.<br>• Offer additional opportunities for learning improvement.<br>• Focus on activities to maximize student choice and prioritize student empowerment and skill building.<br>• Use the "check in" method by inviting students each week to share recent challenges or experiences. Students can "check out" if they do not feel comfortable discussing hardship.<br>• Participate in the discussion so you can "read the class" and observe reactions, emailing students privately to offer additional resources if appropriate.<br>• Use the principles of Transparency in Learning and Teaching (TILT—https://tilthighered.com) to highlight how and why students learn course content in particular ways. TILT helps students understand the relevance of course materials and promotes success. To increase the transparency of your assignments, consider<br>  • adding a section to each assignment explaining how it relates to the objectives of the course;<br>  • identifying a specific learning goal for each assignment;<br>  • spelling out the steps required to complete each assignment;<br>  • detailing how students' work would be evaluated; and<br>  • providing students with annotated examples of past students' work. | Virtual Academic Challenges to Real-Time Trauma (https://fieldeducator.simmons.edu/article/virtual-academic-challenges-to-real-time-trauma)<br><br>Trauma-Informed Care: Core Principle #2 (https://www.centerforebp.case.edu/client-files/events-supportmaterials/2015-0218_TICforR-PHVideoconference.pdf)<br><br>What Is a Trauma-Informed School? (http://safeschoolsnola.tulane.edu/principles-of-trauma-informed-schools)<br><br>Building Trust in Virtual Teams (http://future-thought.pbworks.com/w/file/fetch/118329660/Building_Trust_in_Virtual_Teams.pdf)<br>What Are We Doing and Why? Transparent Assignment Design Benefits Students and Faculty Alike (https://flourishingacademic.wordpress.com/2018/04/16/what-are-we-doing-and-why-transparent-assignment-design-benefits-students-and-faculty-alike)<br><br>A Teaching Intervention That Increases Underserved College Students' Success (https://cte.ku.edu/sites/cte.ku.edu/files/docs/Branding/Winkelmes%20et%20al%202016%20Transparency%20and%20Underserved%20Students.pdf) |

| Principle 3: Facilitate **peer support** | • Facilitate relationship building among your students. Encourage them to check up on each other if appropriate and they are comfortable doing so.<br>• Treat everyone as an equal who shares power and offer students the opportunity to freely choose to engage.<br>• **Classroom peer-support activities:**<br>  • **Formal support group:** Create regularly scheduled discussions where students can offer support through conversation. For example, in Discussions through D2L (or your learning management system), start a forum that asks, "What are current obstacles to online learning? How do you navigate them, and what are your strategies?" Students can then list resources they like best or upload their own study guides to share.<br>  • **Activity-based support:** Create specific online activities so peers can do things together that share a common goal or purpose. Suggesting smaller low-stakes group assignments might be less stressful than big group projects.<br>  • **Learning communities:** Allow students to encounter new material, teach, learn, and submit work together that might have been more difficult to accomplish alone. Google Docs (https://docs.google.com/) provides a space where they collaborate simultaneously in a single document.<br>  • **One-on-one:** Students pair up on their own and more informally throughout the course how they see fit. Introduce them to Google Hangouts (https://hangouts.google.com/) for video calls, available to them through their MyPima emails.<br>  • **Advocacy:** Students and groups decide for themselves "what they want and what changes are required to attain their goal," as well as what resources they need and how to communicate effectively with the right people to make this happen (Blanch et al., 2012, p. 16). They can post their own videos through Loom (https://www.loom.com/), a tool to record themselves and get their message out, instead of writing a long email. | Engaging Women in Trauma- Informed Peer Support (http://www.theannainstitute.org/Andrea%20Blanch%20TTWA/EngagingWomeninTIPeerSupportGuidebook.pdf)<br><br>Peers, More Than Teachers, Inspire Us to Learn (https://msutoday.msu.edu/news/2017/peers-more-than-teachers-inspire-us-to-learn) |

| | | |
|---|---|---|
| Principle 4: Promote **collaboration** | • Create regular opportunities to mutually share information about your and your students' collective situation and personal struggles. <br> • Collect ongoing feedback. Ask your students what matters to them now, what they want to learn, and what interests them. Take notes and incorporate their ideas into your communications and instructions. <br> • Share power with students by inviting them to cocreate assignments. <br> • Offer them tools to work through their feelings. Consider sharing the webinar Stress, Anxiety, Trauma, & Learning; Emotional Regulation for Better Learning (the second reference under Principle 1). <br> • Encourage students to seek peer, family, and community support resources. | Strategies for Collaboration (https://safesupportivelearning.ed.gov/sites/default/files/Building_TSS_Handout_8_collaboration.pdf) <br><br> Trauma Informed Care in the Classroom (https://traumainformedoregon.org/wp-content/uploads/2016/03/Trauma-Informed-Care-in-the-Classroom.pdf) |
| Principle 5: Empower **voice** and **choice** | • Celebrate your students' achievements and encourage them to take pride in their work and themselves. <br> • Validate and normalize student's concerns by talking with your students about fear, stress, anxiety, and trauma. <br> • Provide options regarding course work and different ways to be successful throughout the course. <br> • Inform students if there is an option to "pass" during a discussion or activity should they not feel comfortable participating. <br> • Empower students who have lost a sense of control or agency to have a voice. For example, create a short survey and ask your students, "How can I help you feel empowered during these difficult times?" <br> • Have students practice advocating for themselves and their needs. Applaud their advocacy by listening and working with students to address what they've communicated. <br> • Ensure classroom content reflects the diversity of students in the classroom. | 6 Guiding Principles to a Trauma- Informed Approach (https://www.cdc.gov/cpr/infographics/6_principles_trauma_info.htm) <br><br> Strategies for Collaboration <br><br> Trauma Informed Care in the Classroom |

| Principle 6: Pay attention to **cultural, historical,** and **gender** issues | <ul><li>Understand and use an intersectional lens when considering the challenges your students are facing (see here: https://www.racialequitytools.org/resourcefiles/mapping-margins.pdf).</li><li>Work towards understanding your own default framework and biases related to teaching and learning. "Engage in ongoing self-reflection regarding your own power, privilege, values, history, beliefs, experiences of trauma, etc. to avoid creating the abusive structures that you are trying to dismantle" (Serrata et al., n.d., p. 6).</li><li>Refrain from making assumptions about cultures or groups of people, and instead of justifying a mistake, address its impact and learn from it.</li><li>Incorporate information, practices, and voices that have been historically disregarded or excluded in your discipline.</li><li>Implement accessible and equitable teaching and learning strategies. For example, consider an assessment framework that is focused less on grading and more on learning improvement and celebration of learning. See 7 Exam Questions for a Pandemic: https://www.francissu.com/post/7-exam-questions-for-a-pandemic-or-any-other-time.</li><li>Invite discussion on more nuanced issues of accessibility in the online environment. Allow students to occupy the online class in ways that allow them to feel comfortable (breaks during synchronous lectures, less screen time, not having to share their camera, etc.)</li><li>Embrace cultural wellness and wisdom. For example, provide opportunities to share a tradition or value from where students draw strength. Also, both students and faculty can identify daily wellness strategies in order to prevent burnout, vicarious trauma, and secondary trauma (Serrata et al., p. 5).</li></ul> | 6 Guiding Principles to a Trauma-Informed Approach<br><br>Margaret Price, "Un/Shared Space," in Disability, Space, Architecture: A Reader, ed. by Jos Boys (New York: Routledge, 2017).<br><br>Responding to Racial Bias and Microaggressions in Online Environments (https://www.youtube.com/watch?v=9cEWQJ32nqU)<br><br>Trauma Informed Principles through a Culturally Specific Lens (http://nationallatinonetwork.org/images/Trauma-Informed-Principles-through-a-Culturally-Specific-Lens_FINAL.pdf)<br><br><ul><li>Virtual Academic Challenges to Real-Time Trauma (https://www2.simmons.edu/ssw/fe/i/16-141.pdf)</li></ul> |

101 |

**References**

Blanch, A., Filson, B., Penney, D., & Cave, C. (2012, April). *Engaging women in trauma-informed peer support: A guidebook.* National Center for Trauma-Informed Care. http://www.theannainstitute.org/Andrea%20 Blanch%20TIWA/EngagingWomeninTIPeerSupportGuidebook.pdf

Serrata, J., Notario, H., & Ortega, V. P. (n.d.). *Trauma informed principles through a culturally specific lens.* https://nationallatinonetwork.org/images/ Trauma-Informed-Principles-through-a-Culturally-Specific-Lens_FINAL. pdf

# PART 3

# RESOURCES
# FOR
# STUDENTS

# Planning for Success in Remote, Hybrid, and Online Classes: A Handout for Students

*Wren Mills*

I advise a fraternity on my campus, and in early August, several of the officers came to me concerned about how to keep students on track academically this year. Their main worry was most students' lack of interest in a fully online educational experience. The students consistently reported that they'd found the spring shift to remote and hybrid learning to be, at the very least, challenging. And this fall many of them have found themselves in exactly the same situation with all online courses—a situation that may continue next spring. I suspect those concerns are shared by students around the country. I've been teaching online and hybrid courses for 15 years, and my students have offered some very helpful advice about learning successfully in that modality. I decided to share some of their insights in handout that could be posted online or given out. Feel free to share it with your students. If you need to adapt it, that's fine too.

**For classes meeting remotely**

On days when you'll meet via Zoom or some other web-conferencing program, **do your best to have a place where you can be focused and comfortable**. I know this can be hard, especially for those of you who are at home, sharing spaces and technology with the rest of the family, but doing so will enable you to get more out of the session. Keep in mind that comfort (sitting up on your bed) might not result in focus!

If you are at home, **look for a quiet place so it will be easy to focus**. This might be a closet! Lots of journalists have had to do this for their work over the last few months, and it can work for you too!

**Sitting at an actual table or desk really helps**. This makes it easy to access to your computer, textbook, notes, etc. When I decide to work in the living room, I have a portable card table that I use, for example.

**Do your best to have decent internet access**. Last semester, some of my students told me they'd go to parking lots on campus or to a campus nearby to access the Wi-Fi. They'd sit in their back seats for "class," and if they had Bluetooth in their cars, they'd let that sound system pump out the sound. Be sure to let your instructors know if you do NOT have a good internet connection and might need to turn off video or might be seen logging in repeatedly because you've been dropped.

**Keep unneeded apps and windows and tabs closed**. I know the temptation—I do it myself during some Zoom meetings—but it's easier to resist if you don't see the program open on your task bar.

**If your professor gives you the chance to stand up, move or take a break—take it!** The brain can process only what the butt on the chair can withstand. Plus, it resets your attention span and will freshen your memory capabilities a bit.

I know you'll be at a computer or on your tablet or phone, but there is SO MUCH research that shows that **note-taking on paper helps you commit information to memory better than taking digital notes**. This is because of the way your brain works, and you're not going to change that hardwiring. So, notes on paper mean less studying in the long run.

### For online classes

My new-to-online students tell me this is the single most helpful piece of advice that I ever give them: **If your class is 100 percent online, schedule it into your life in two to three blocks of 60–90 minutes each week like you would an in-person class. And make yourself "go to class" during those times**. Be consistent. Don't move that time block around. If you finish up your work for the week before your time blocks are used up, great! Take a literal break from school—you earned it.

If your professor uses Blackboard calendar or provides a schedule, download or print it (or both) and use it as a checklist so you don't forget important course details.

I recommend that you **keep your own calendar**—a Google Calendar, an Outlook calendar, any app you like! Put in the big and little things—all things count in a course. Let it buzz your phone to remind you of due dates and to keep you from procrastinating.

**For any class**

Remember that regardless of whether it is your first semester or your last, **this is not a "normal" semester**. There are lots of new stresses, and even if you aren't too worried about staying healthy, somewhere in the back of your brain, avoiding getting the virus, staying healthy, and hoping your family stays healthy could be causing you stress. With that in mind, **you might have to do different things to keep your routine**, especially if you're living at home and not on campus or in an apartment. A different routine makes it easy to make mistakes you wouldn't normally make.

**Consider keeping all your school stuff in one place, and keep it there consistently so you don't misplace it and end up stressed about that**. This doesn't mean you can't work on the back porch or at Starbucks, but as soon as you are back home, put your stuff in its place. I had to take this advice myself—I kept losing things between my home office, the kitchen, the covered back porch, and the living room. Now I have three milk crates in the office where stuff goes: one for classes I'm teaching (books, binders, folders); one for committee work (notebooks and folders); and one for all my supplies. My crates stack up neatly, and I can keep the cats out of them. Find what works for you!

**If you aren't sure about something in the course, ask**. Many on-line courses (and hybrids that use Blackboard) will have an "Ask a Question"-type discussion board—just email the instructor. Be sure to check the syllabus for the answer first, and be aware of what your professor's policy is on answering emails (some don't check on the weekend, for example), but by all means ask.

**Talk to your peers. Find out what has and hasn't worked for them**. If this is your first semester in college or your first time in an online course, ask classmates who are more experienced with online and hybrid classes. They will have good student perspectives on what worked and didn't work. Many of your instructors haven't been students for a while.

**Closing thoughts**

**Be forgiving of your instructors, your peers, and yourself this semester**. While some faculty on campus have been teaching online for a long time, for others it's a brand-new experience. They are learning to navigate this new world just like you are. This is the same for your classmates; some are old hands at online learning, and for others it's a brave new world. So give yourself a break. You aren't the only one stressed out and making mistakes. We're all in this together. Remember this as you, your classmates, and your teachers work to learn online: a deep breath, some kindness, and a little patience can go a long way!

> Visit this link to download an editable Word version of this handout:
> https://s26600.pcdn.co/wp-content/uploads/2020/09/Succeeding-in-Online-Courses-Handout-1.docx

# A Memo to Students on Punching through the Pandemic

*Regan A. R. Gurung*

Dear Students,

Confused by remote learning? Uncertain? Anxious? Worried? Stressed? Unclear what next week will bring? For many of us faculty, the answer to all these is yes. I am guessing that many of you are experiencing this as well. We are all in this together. Your faculty and schools have your back. Here are some ways to better navigate the weeks ahead as colleges and universities across the nation move instruction online.

**What does this mean for you?** Learning online can be challenging in general and especially if it is new to you, but there are positives and many strategies and resources to help you learn well online. Instructors will vary in how they approach "remote teaching," our term for delivering classes over the web. For some of you, classes will not be limited to set times of the day or week. Many classes will change format so that you can access the lectures of materials more on your schedule. You may be stressed because not all your remote classes will be the same and you will have to navigate the differences. We faculty know that and like clarity and certainty too, so whether we meet at a fixed (synchronous) or flexible (asynchronous) time, your instructors will work to make sure meetings times, assignments, and expectations are clear. You will know exactly what happens when, just like in your face-to-courses. If you are unsure, contact your instructor immediately.

Classes may also change so that the format of tests and assignments varies. If your class would have had a lot of multiple-choice exams, it may have more discussion boards and short essay assignments that give you better (and less stressful) ways interact with the material and show what you know.

Going remote may also allow you even more interaction with your classmates. That's because a course on a learning management system (LMS), such as Canvas or Blackboard, has many technological bells and whistles to give you more ways to learn that an in-person lecture does.

**There may be delays**. While many of you have not taken online classes, many faculty have not taught online either. This makes remote learning even tougher. Our commitment to your education is motivating us to hustle and get our courses online even if we have never taught online before. Even with very hard work, going online still takes time. What faculty are being asked to do on short notice is unique. Teaching remotely is a safety feature to reduce exposure; it is the easiest way to continue to educate without shutting down and delaying your graduation. Teaching remotely is not the same as teaching an online class. Remote teaching is an instant response to an emergent health crisis and is being set up quickly. In contrast, online teaching involves the same planning, energy, and investment that goes into teaching in person, and both use evidence-based teaching. While we are using the many best practices for online teaching to guide your remote learning, be prepared for a lot of trial and error.

*If you do not hear back from your instructor about an upcoming class or they have not responded to your email(s), be patient.* Give your professors some leeway. They are trying hard to get up to speed and just need some time. They want to do the best job for you that they can, and this is not easy right now. They'll be cutting you some slack in adjusting to this situation as well.

**How can you best prepare? GET TECHY**. If you have never taken a class online before, take the time to get familiar with how it works. All schools are creating resources for you. Here are two great ones from Oregon State: Learning Online (https://success.oregonstate.edu/learning/learning-online) and Keep Learning (https://learn.oregonstate.edu/keep-learning). These will give you basic technology savviness—and some great tips for learning online as well. Tech savvy, after all, isn't everything.

When courses are all online, a lot more of the responsibility is in YOUR HANDS. You have to make sure you find the time to log in for each of your courses. You now have readings, assignments, and discussions for multiple courses with no in-person time when the instructor will remind you of what is due when. **PLAN WELL** (https://success.oregonstate.edu/build-your-time-management-toolbox). Create a schedule for the next few weeks, blocking out when you will work on which class. Yes, this is a good thing to do in general, but now it becomes a critical need to stay sane and on top of it all.

One very important reminder: **TAKE NOTES** (https://success.oregonstate.edu/sites/success.oregonstate.edu/files/LearningCorner/

Tools/4-page_note_taking_20.pdf). While 98 percent of students take notes while in face-to-face classes, few take notes in online classes. If all your classes are online, you may think you have a lot of extra time or that you can take a break from note-taking. Bad idea. Even if your remote teaching instructor does not do synchronous lectures, take notes on the recorded lectures and your reading assignments. Notes keep you focused and help you learn.

**ATTEND to your mental and physical health**. By now you know to keep your distance, wash your hands often, and not touch your face, but social distancing is a poor choice of term. Keep physical distance but play UP your social ties. Talk to, text, and message your friends and family. Keep in touch. Reconnect. Social support is one of the biggest psychological predictors of health. If you need information or emotional support, prioritize getting it. Make special time for friends and ensure you get physical activity. This is also the time to sleep more. Eating well, sleeping more, and talking to friends are all factors that will make your body stronger at fending off infection and speed up your recovery if you do get sick.

**REACH OUT** if you need help. Key services such as Student Success, Advising, and Counseling (or the equivalent on your campus) are working to make sure they can deliver their services remotely as well. They can be your first stop for support as you navigate this new experience. These offices will have many things available, just in different formats.

I absolutely adore teaching in person, and I know many of you love going to a physical class and interacting with your classmates in real life. The energy that arises from the learning process is palpable. Teaching online can have a lot of that too. Many students do as well in well-designed online classes as they do in person—sometimes better. That is good to know. I have taught online and loved it. Students learned. It was still a hard transition the first time. And I had a lot of time to make it. Regular online teaching is not the same as remote teaching, but we both should be open to doing things in new ways. You can still learn well, but you'll have to change your expectations.

The faculty and staff at your universities know how stressful this can be for you. Do not hesitate to reach out to us. Together we will punch through this pandemic.

Sincerely,

Your Professor

Visit this link to download an editable Word version of this
handout:
https://www.teachingprofessor.com/wp-content/uploads/2021/03/
A-Memo-to-Students-on-Punching-through-the-Pandemic.docx

# Adapting for 2021: A Student's Guide

*Regan A. R. Gurung*

Dear Student,

Fall 2020 is in the books. How did it go?

Few residential students looked forward to the thought of another term of remote learning or socially distanced face-to-face classes. It is just not the same thing taking a class scattered around a large room, masked, and following arrows and signs to keep space at every turn. Remote learning, with its umpteen hours spent in the same room staring at the same screen day in and day out, was not a much rosier enterprise either. Even online learning was tough.

Add to that being unable to socialize or see family to the same extent as before the pandemic, health concerns, homeschooling children, caring for unwell family, coping with job loss/changes, and experiencing a volatile year rife with political and racial unrest.

Psychological science suggests that when we have little control over an issue, when stressors are unpredictable, and when they are long term (all characteristics of the pandemic), it is best to activate additional coping responses. By now you have heard about the importance of having social support, getting extra sleep, eating well, and getting physical exercise. In preparation for the new year ahead, the end of the fall is a great time to reflect on what worked well and what needs to change. Here are some helpful tips culled from research and student feedback.

**Condition yourself**. Physical classrooms, the buildings they are in, and campus condition us for learning. We associate each with "being in class." This link helps us switch into "academic mode." If all your learning is now taking place in the same room or at the same table, then you need to develop new stimuli to differentiate the activities you partake in in that space. Create cues to get your mind learning. Examples include placing your class books in clear view only during class times and not playing any music or having the TV on when you are in class. It could even be throwing on a specific jacket when you are in class (i.e., a Zoom shirt). Anything that will signal to your brain that you are in class rather than not is good.

Do not forget reward and punishment. Work for a set period (e.g., one hour) and then reward yourself (e.g., watch a show) after you do. Likewise, if you do not get work done as scheduled, withhold a pleasurable activity that you would otherwise engage in.

**Keep your routine**. If you built in time to get ready for class and commute to school, try keeping the same schedule. Yes, the trip to your computer is much shorter, but use time saved to get things done. Dressing up like you would if you were going to a physical class surrounded by people and being seen gives your body a slight physiological kick that can help you pay attention better. Set your alarms as if you had face-to-face classes. The signs of normalcy can help.

**Change your routine (if it failed)**. Many students had a routine that involved sleeping in, not changing for class, and doing all their work in one spot. They reported this did not work well. If what you did in fall 2020 did not work for you, change it. We sometimes get stuck in a rut and a change can bring novelty and increase our motivation. Try including specific NEW routines—such as taking a walk and getting air before an afternoon class or preparing your favorite snack before a challenging class. Factor in seasonal changes in the weather, too, and be prepared for changes due to harsh winters.

**Tighten your schedule**. Scheduling is even more important during the pandemic. Plan everything; setting time for fun and for work and allows both to get done. Even put solo "you" time and sitting (or strolling, walking, hiking, running, or bike riding) outside on your checklist so you get air, a change of pace, and some mindfulness. Then make sure you do it and check it off. MOST importantly, schedule even asynchronous classes. Students who set aside time to work on class (regardless of whether it was live or recorded) got work done.

**Un-divide your attention**. The single biggest change you can make is to ensure that your attention is undivided. Checking social media or surfing websites in a separate window may seem to make a tough class bearable but defeats the purpose of your being there. If the class chat is distracting, switch it off. Even simply turning your phone off is not enough. Put it in a different room to make it hard to get to easily. Even briefly checking your phone can disrupt your focus. You may start for a quick look, but that may be hard to stop, and you may get sucked in. Before you know if, you decide to log out of class. It happened. Often. Watch for it.

**Take notes**. Even if participating in class from your room, take notes as if you were in a physical classroom. This is even important if you only have recorded lectures to watch or all asynchronous work. Taking notes organizes your learning and increases retention.

**Turn your camera ON**. Students reported that having their cameras on helped them stay focused in class and made it less likely for them to distract themselves with phones or step away to do other things. It made them feel like they were IN a face-to-face class. Seeing other classmates felt good, and the game face they felt they had to wear helped with their own attention too. While bandwidth problems or not having your own space may preclude this, IF YOU CAN, turn on your camera.

We all want the pandemic to end, but it will be some time before learning as usual resumes. In the meantime forearm yourself to make the best of another round of remote learning.

Sincerely,

Your Professor

Visit this link to download an editable Word version of this handout:
https://www.teachingprofessor.com/wp-content/uploads/2021/03/Adapting-for-2021_A-Students-Guide.docx

# About the Contributors

**Bridget Arend**, PhD, is the owner of Intentional College Teaching and is affiliate faculty and the former executive director of the Office of Teaching and Learning at the University of Denver. She has 20 years of experience supporting teaching and learning in higher education.

**Joseph Bentz**, PhD, is a professor of English and an Honors College faculty fellow at Azusa Pacific University, where he teaches courses in writing and literature. His emphasis is 20th-century American literature, and much of his scholarly work has focused on novelist Thomas Wolfe.

**Linda M. Boland**, PhD, is a professor of biology and director of the Teaching and Scholarship Hub at the University of Richmond in Virginia. During the pandemic, she helped prepare faculty for teaching using videoconferencing technology, which she also used in her own fall term teaching.

**Samantha Clifford**, EdD, is assistant dean of online and innovative educational initiatives and adjunct professor with Northern Arizona University. Dr. Clifford has a multidisciplinary background in psychology, anthropology, and education. She has worked in the areas of instructional design, faculty professional development, academic student success, and international education.

**Madeline Craig**, EdD, is an assistant professor of education and the dual-degree program coordinator at Molloy College in New York. Her research interests include the use of instructional technology in higher education and K–12, project-based learning, improvement of students' writing skills, and technology integration for teacher candidates and faculty.

**Jon Crylen**, PhD, is editor of online publications for Magna Publications. His writing, which focuses on environmental film and media, has appeared in the *Journal of Cinema and Media Studies*, *Media Fields Journal*, *Cinema of Exploration: Essays on an Adventurous Film Practice* (Routledge), and *A Cultural History of the Sea in the Modern Age* (Bloomsbury Academic).

**Nichole DeWall**, PhD, is a professor of English at McKendree University in Lebanon, Illinois. She teaches medieval and early modern literature as well as drama and composition courses. Her research focuses on teaching Shakespeare and representations of disease in early modern drama.

**Robert S. Fleming**, EdD, is a professor of management in the Rowan University Rohrer College of Business, where he previously served as dean. He has an affiliate appointment as a professor of crisis and emergency management.

**Regan A. R. Gurung**, PhD, is a professor of psychological science, the director of the General Psychology program, and the interim executive director for the Center for Teaching and Learning at Oregon State University. Follow him on Twitter @ReganARGurung.

**Mays Imad**, PhD, is a neuroscientist and professor of pathophysiology and biomedical ethics at Pima Community College, the founding coordinator of the Teaching and Learning Center, and a John N. Gardner Institute Fellow. Follow her on Twitter @lrningsanctuary.

**Sami Lange**, MLIS, MSEd, serves as academic engagement and open education librarian at Paradise Valley Community College. She is the former chair of the World Languages Department at Santa Rosa Junior College.

**Eric D. Loepp**, PhD, is an assistant professor of political science at the University of Wisconsin–Whitewater, where he teaches courses in American government, political behavior, and research methods. His pedagogical interests center on data- and technology-enhanced teaching techniques.

**Claire Howell Major**, PhD, is a professor of higher education administration at the University of Alabama. Her work focuses on teaching and learning, and she has published several books and articles with this focus, including *Teaching Online: A Guide to Theory, Research, and Practice*.

**Wren Mills**, PhD, is a pedagogical assistant professor in the Department of Educational Administration, Leadership, and Research at Western Kentucky University.

**Katie E. O'Leary** is an instructor of English at South Dakota State University.

**John Orlando**, PhD, is an education consultant who has spent over 20 years developing and growing educational programs at a variety of colleges and universities as well as teaching faculty how to be great instructors both online and in face-to-face classrooms. He writes and edits articles on online teaching and learning for *The Teaching Professor.*

**Jessica Pardoe** is the former chair of the English as a Second Language Department at Santa Rosa Junior College.

**Dave Pursell**, PhD, is professor of chemistry and environmental science at Georgia Gwinnett College and has taught in all areas of chemistry, environmental law, military strategy, and advanced technologies in military operations. He served worldwide as a US Army combat engineer for 25 years before transitioning to higher education.

**Lisa C. Schumaier**, MFA, is a writing adjunct professor and fellow for the Teaching and Learning Center at Pima Community College. She is also the author Dot Devota, whose books include *The Division of Labor* (Rescue Press), *And the Girls Worried Terribly* (Noemi Press), *The Eternal Wall* (Book*hug), and *The Dept. of Posthumous Letters* (Argos Books).

**Lauren Tucker**, EdD, is an assistant professor of special education and coordinator of the assistive technology program at Southern Connecticut State University. Dr. Tucker has expertise in assistive technology, UDL, online learning, and technology implementation. Dr. Tucker leads trainings for integrating UDL, online learning, and other topics to enhance teaching practice.

**Maryellen Weimer**, PhD, has served as editor of *The Teaching Professor* since the newsletter began in 1987. She is a professor emerita of teaching and learning at Penn State Berks and won Penn State's Milton S. Eisenhower Award for distinguished teaching in 2005.

# Additional Resources

**Additional Resources from Magna Publications**

## BULK PURCHASES

To purchase multiple print copies of this book, please contact Magna Sales at sales@magnapubs.com or call 800-433-0499 ext. 183.

## MEMBERSHIPS/SUBSCRIPTIONS

### *Faculty Focus*

www.facultyfocus.com
A free e-newsletter on effective teaching strategies for the college classroom.

### The Teaching Professor Membership

www.TeachingProfessor.com
The Teaching Professor is an annual membership that reflects the changing needs of today's college faculty and the students they teach. This new fully online version of the newsletter that faculty have enjoyed for more than 30 years includes the best of the print version—great articles and practical, evidence-based insights—but also many new features including video, graphics, and links that make it an even more indispensable resource.

### Academic Leader Membership

www.Academic-Leader.com
Academic Leader covers the trends, challenges, and best practices today's academic decision-makers. Members gain access to the latest thinking in academic leadership and learn how peers at other institutions are solving problems, managing change, and setting direction. New articles are published throughout the month.

## CONFERENCES

### The Teaching Professor Conference

www.TeachingProfessorConference.com

This event provides an opportunity to learn effective pedagogical techniques, hear from leading teaching experts, and interact with colleagues committed to teaching and learning excellence. Join more than 1,000 educators from around the country. Attendees hear from a roster of prestigious experts and nationally recognized thought leaders. A broad mix of plenary addresses, concurrent sessions, and timely roundtable discussions leave no topic untouched.

### Leadership in Higher Education Conference

www.AcademicLeadershipConference.com

The Leadership in Higher Education Conference provides higher-education leaders with an opportunity to expand leadership skills with proactive strategies, engaging networking, time-saving tips, and best practices.

## BOOKS

### *The Academic Leader's Handbook: A Resource Collection for College Administrators*

https://www.amazon.com/dp/B0764KMC5Z

*The Academic Leader's Handbook: A Resource Collection for College Administrators* details an array of proven management strategies and will help further your achievements as a leader in higher education. Discover new leadership tools and insights at departmental, administrative, and executive levels.

### *Active Learning: A Practical Guide for College Faculty*

https://www.amazon.com/dp/B071ZN8R32

Learn how to apply active learning methods in both small and large classes as well as in an online teaching environment. Whether you are new to active learning methods or experienced with them, this comprehensive reference book can guide you every step of the way.

### *The College Teacher's Handbook: A Resource Collection for New Faculty*

https://www.amazon.com/dp/0912150688

*The College Teacher's Handbook: A Resource Collection for New Faculty* provides the essential tools and information that any new teacher in higher education needs to confidently lead a college classroom.

### *Essential Teaching Principles: A Resource Collection for Adjunct Faculty*
https://www.amazon.com/dp/0912150246
This book provides a wealth of both research-driven and classroom-tested best practices to help adjuncts develop the knowledge and skills required to run a successful classroom. Compact and reader-friendly, this book is conveniently organized to serve as a ready reference whenever a new teaching challenge arises—whether it's refreshing older course design, overcoming a student's objection to a grade, or fine-tuning assessments.

### *Essential Teaching Principles: A Resource Collection for Teachers*
https://www.amazon.com/dp/0912150580
This book serves as a quick and ready reference as you encounter the challenges of teaching college-level material in the high school classroom. For an AP or IB teacher, there's no better resource.

### *Faculty Development: A Resource Collection for Academic Leaders*
https://www.amazon.com/dp/0912150661
Discover proven tips and insights, from top academic experts, that will help you enhance faculty development programming and training on your campus.

### *Flipping the College Classroom: Practical Advice from Faculty*
https://www.amazon.com/dp/B01N2GZ61O
This collection is a comprehensive guide to flipping no matter how much—or how little—experience you have with it. If you are just getting started, you will learn where and how to begin. If you have been at it for a while, you will find new ideas to try and solutions to common challenges. *Flipping the College Classroom: Practical Advice from Faculty* is an invaluable resource that covers all the necessary territory.

### *Grading Strategies for the Online College Classroom: A Collection of Articles for Faculty*
https://www.amazon.com/dp/0912150564
Do your grading practices accurately reflect your online students' performance? Do your assessment and feedback methods inspire learning? Are you managing the time you spend on these things—or is the workload overwhelming? *Grading Strategies for the Online College Classroom: A Collection of Articles for Faculty* can help you master the techniques of effective online grading—while avoiding some of the more costly pitfalls.

**Helping Students Learn: Resources, Tools, and Activities for College Educators**
https://www.amazon.com/dp/0912150602
This workbook is a must-have guide for faculty. While the roles in the college classroom often are defined by teachers teaching and students learning, the reality is that not many students have a clear understanding of how to learn.

**Leading through Crisis, Conflict, and Change in Higher Education**
https://www.amazon.com/dp/0912150769
*Leading through Crisis, Conflict, and Change in Higher Education* brings you direct advice, from qualified subject matter experts from a variety of campuses, on wide-ranging nuanced aspects of managing difficult issues and topics. Make this your tool for discovering the multiple facets of crisis communication, conflict management, and change leadership in higher education.

**Managing Adjunct Faculty: A Resource Collection for Administrators**
https://www.amazon.com/dp/B01N2OVK5W
Chances are your adjunct population has been built on an ad hoc basis to fill instructional needs. As a result, your institution might not have a solid management framework to support them. That's a gap you can close with guidance from *Managing Adjunct Faculty: A Resource Collection for Administrators*. This invaluable guide offers an extensive review of best practices for managing an adjunct cohort and integrating them more fully into your campus community.

**The New Dean's Survival Guide: Advice from an Academic Leader**
https://www.amazon.com/dp/091215070X
Find numerous tools and strategies to address challenges, successes, and issues leaders face with this comprehensive survival guide with advice for deans, provosts, and managers in higher education.

**Planning and Designing Your College Course**
https://www.amazon.com/dp/B088W1WX9K
*Planning and Designing Your College Course* focuses on the planning aspects that precede the launching of a course—the work instructors do behind the scenes and that students usually aren't privy to. You'll be able to make each key part of your course design learner-centered and obtain strategies to get students to collaborate in the course design process.

***Teaching Strategies for the Online College Classroom: A Collection of Faculty Articles***

https://www.amazon.com/dp/0912150483

Includes online teaching strategies ranging from building a successful start of the semester, fostering productive connections, managing challenging behavior in the online classroom, and enhancing student engagement.

# Bonus Content!

## Eight Steps for a Smoother Transition to Online Teaching

*by J. A. Miller*

## Online Discussions: Five Kinds of Forums

*by Maryellen Weimer*

## The Need for Pragmatic Expectations in Online Courses

*by Stephanie Smith Budhai*

## Sign up at

https://magnapubs.lpages.co/remote-teaching-and-learning-book-bonus/
to access these articles

Made in the USA
Middletown, DE
25 April 2021